PASSOVER

ITS HISTORY AND TRADITIONS

PASSOVER

ITS HISTORY AND TRADITIONS

by

Theodor Herzel Gaster

ABELARD-SCHUMAN

LONDON AND NEW YORK

Printed in U.S.A. and bound in Great Britain by
Webb, Son and Co., Ltd., London, E.C.1, for
Abelard-Schuman Limited
38 Russell Square, London, W.C.1

To the One
Who Is Too Young
to Ask

CONTENTS

	FOREWORD	9
1	WHAT PASSOVER IS	13
2	HOW PASSOVER BEGAN	16
3	ISRAEL IN EGYPT	26
4	FOLKLORE IN THE BIBLE STORY	40
5	PASSOVER LEGENDS OF THE JEWS	46
6	THE SEDER	52
7	SONGS OF THE SEDER	67
8	MORE PASSOVER SONGS	73
9	THE SAMARITAN PASSOVER	77
10	DEW	84
11	THE SONG OF SONGS	87
	EPILOGUE	93
	BIBLIOGRAPHY	95
	INDEX	99

ILLUSTRATIONS

Celebration of the Passover 23

Seti I, the Pharaoh of the Oppression 33

Ramesses II, the Pharaoh of the Exodus 33

Medieval Conception of Pithom and Raamses 34

The Route of the Exodus 37

Moses Wields the Magic Rod 48

The Removal of Leaven 53

Celebration of the Seder 56

The Four Sons 59

Who Knows Three? The Three Patriarchs: Abraham, Isaac, and Jacob 70

Who Knows Four? The Four Matriarchs: Sarah, Rebekah, Leah, and Rachel 70

Then Came the Holy One, Blessed Be He, and Slew the Angel of Death 72

Samaritans Slaughtering the Pascal Lamb 80

FOREWORD

THERE are many books about Passover, describing its rites and ceremonies and relating its customs and traditions. This book tries to do something more. It tries to tell the story of the festival not only in terms of the accepted tradition but also against the background of modern knowledge. It seeks to present to the inquiring layman the full story of what recent research has to say about the true origins of Passover, the parallels to it in various parts of the world, and the historical authenticity of the events which it commemorates.

Against this wider background, the real nature and significance of the festival stand out in a clearer light. It is seen to reflect in the successive stages of its development those of Man's elemental quest for Freedom. It starts as a festival of *physical* freedom—a crude and primitive ceremony designed to free men, from year to year, from the hurt and hazard of life and the mischief of Nature. It develops into a festival of *social* freedom, commemorating the liberation of a particular people from bondage. And it ends—if end it does—as a festival of *human* freedom, celebrating the ideal of Liberty itself, of which that liberation is but a symbol.

If the festival is compact of hopes and fears, it is also replete with imagination and fancy. The ideals which it brings into focus stem not only from the head but also from the heart, and find expression not only in rite and precept but also in poetry and legend. The quaint elaborations and embellishments which have delighted the observant throughout the ages and which have now become part and parcel of the festival are therefore also included in this volume.

At the same time, it must be borne in mind that this is a popular work, not an exhaustive encyclopaedia, and that limitations of space have curtailed the discussion of some minor details. Those who wish for more information on this or that particular topic may be referred to the Bibliography, where further literature is indicated. Our purpose here has been to paint a broad picture of Passover as interpreted especially in the light of ancient history and comparative religion and folklore.

It must be remembered that all research is, as William James puts it, "subject to the better insight of the morrow." Our knowledge of the remote past increases with new discoveries from day to day, so that the conclusions at which scholars have arrived on the basis of material at present available may have to be modified in the future. To quote James again, "We can be right, at any moment, only 'up to date' and 'on the whole.'"

PASSOVER
ITS HISTORY AND
TRADITIONS

1

WHAT PASSOVER IS

Passover is one of the oldest festivals in the world. It has been observed by Jews, with unbroken regularity, for more than three thousand years.

The festival falls in spring, in the first month of the Hebrew year, called Nisan (March-April), and lasts for eight days, from the fifteenth to the twenty-third. It marks the beginning of the barley season in Palestine and at the same time commemorates the deliverance of the Israelites from Egypt and the fact that God *passed over* their houses when He smote the first-born in that land. For the latter reason, it is known among Jews as "the season of our liberation."

Passover was not always what it is today. In Biblical times, it was distinguished by a far more primitive ceremonial.

Between dusk and dark, on the fourteenth day of the month, each household publicly slaughtered a yearling lamb or goat, selected four days earlier. Then they took of its blood and smeared it with a bunch of hyssop on the doorposts and lintels of their dwellings.

At night, in the light of the full moon, each family consumed the slaughtered beast, roasted whole, together with unleavened bread (*matzah*) and bitter herbs. The meal had to be eaten in haste, and nothing was permitted to remain over in the morning. What was not eaten had to be burned.

The eating of unleavened bread continued for seven days, during which period all leavened food was forbidden. The entire celebration, as distinct from the paschal meal alone, was therefore known popularly as the Feast of Unleavened Bread.

Among the Israelites, this ancient, time-honored festival came to acquire a new meaning. It was, so the story ran, on Passover night that their ancestors had departed from the bondage of Egypt; and it was just because they had so religiously observed the rite of smearing blood on their doorposts that God had been able to recognize their houses and spare them when he smote the first-born in that land. The festival was therefore continued as a perpetual reminder of that great deliverance.

Every detail of the ceremonial was related to this. The haste with which the paschal meal was eaten commemorated the hasty departure from Egypt; and the unleavened bread recalled the fact that the people had no time to bake their loaves properly, but "took their dough before it was leavened." As for the name of the festival, this was readily explained: had not God *passed over* the homes of His people on that memorable night?

In later times, when public worship in Israel came to be concentrated in the Temple, families living near Jerusalem brought their paschal lambs to that spot to be slaughtered, those unable to do so being allowed to postpone the ceremony for one month.

In 70 A.D., however, the Temple was destroyed, and sacrifices came to an end. The paschal rite therefore fell into abeyance. But the consumption of unleavened bread was continued; and, as a memorial of the ancient rite, it was eaten especially, together with bitter herbs, at a home ceremony on the evening of the fourteenth day of the month. At the same time, the story of the Exodus (tricked out, in course of time, with fanciful explanations, psalms, prayers, and secular songs) was duly recited.

This is the manner in which the festival is observed today. The home ceremony is called the *Seder*—a Hebrew word meaning "order of service"; while the accompanying recital is known as the *Haggadah*, or "story"—a name derived from the words of the Biblical commandment: "On that day thou shalt tell the story to thy son, saying, This is because of that which the LORD did for me when I came forth out of Egypt" (Exodus 13:8).

Later ages also introduced another important change in the observance of the festival. Originally, it had been kept for seven days. Now an eighth was added. The reason for this was that in ancient times the dates of festivals were determined by the occurrence of the preceding new moon, and this was announced to outlying communities by relay messengers or fire-signals sent out by the central authorities in Jerusalem. Since these could not always reach their destination in time, an extra day was added in order to make sure that the one proclaimed by the authorities would in any case be observed.

Orthodox and Conservative Jews living outside of Palestine have retained this custom. Reform Jews, however, have discarded it, reverting to the original Biblical system.

2

HOW PASSOVER BEGAN

PASSOVER was already an established institution at the time the Israelites came out of Egypt. The Bible itself implies as much. For what it tells is not how the festival began but how it came to be preserved. Its previous existence is taken for granted, and the narrative seeks only to rationalize its survival in terms of Israel's particular history.

What the Israelite writers were doing was simply what men have always done when the garment of custom begins to wear thin and when the real meaning of a traditional institution is no longer remembered. They were doing, in fact, precisely what the English do today when they interpret the traditional Battle between Summer and Winter—still performed in several parts of the country—as a memorial of the fight between Christian ("Saint George") and Saracen ("Turkish Knight") at the time of the Crusades, or even, more grotesquely, of that between King George the Third and Napoleon!

Yet beneath the historical veneer it is not difficult to detect the contours of an older and more primitive pattern. What the ancient writers did not know, modern scholars can supply. For the fact is that when the historical explanations are stripped away, the rites and ceremonies of Passover as described in the Bible find parallels in many parts of the world and fall into a pattern characteristic of primitive seasonal rituals.

The central feature of the entire ceremonial was, as we have seen, a common meal eaten by all members of a family at full moon in the first month of the year. According to the Israelite writers, anyone who abstained was deemed to have "cut himself off from his people."

Now, such eating together is a standard method, all over the world, of establishing ties of kinship or alliance, the idea being that a common substance and essence is thereby absorbed. Indeed, our own word *companion* means properly *one who shares bread with* another; while the Gaelic word for "family," viz., *cuedich,* denotes those who *eat together.*

A few examples must suffice. Among the Kumis of Southeast India, alliances are made by killing a goat, eating it in common, and smearing its blood on the participants. In the Papuan villages of Leti, Moa, and Lakor, friendship is established with neighboring communities by eating common flesh and drinking common blood. In Madagascar, brotherhood is produced by drinking out of the same bowl. Among the Timorlaut, bonds of mutual assistance are created by killing a slave and eating him jointly; while in the Watubella Islands and among the people of Luang-Sermata, reconciliation is effected after quarrels—as so often among ourselves—by drinking together. Similarly, Herodotus informs us that among the Nasamoneans of Libya "the manner of concluding a treaty was that each party gave the other to drink out of his hand"; and, to this day, it is standard Arab custom that anyone who has eaten the smallest morsel of your food—in some cases, even if he has stolen it—is entitled to your aid and protection.

Nor was the custom unknown in Biblical times; it is

not infrequently mentioned in Scripture. Thus, when Melchizedek, King of Salem, made a treaty with Abraham, he did so by proffering bread and wine (Genesis 14:18-24); and when Abimelech concluded an alliance with Isaac, he followed the same procedure (Genesis 26:30). Similarly, we are told expressly in the Book of Joshua (9:14) that the princes of Israel entered into a covenant with the Gibeonites by partaking of their victuals; and the prophet Obadiah (verse 7) uses the words "men of thy bread" and "men of thy confederacy" as parallel expressions for the same thing.

We may take it, then, that *the original purpose of the paschal meal was to recement ties of kinship, infuse new life into the family, and renew the bonds of mutual protection at the beginning of each year.*

In a ceremony of this kind, it is not only how you eat but also what you eat that is important. For it is from the flesh which is eaten that the common life is renewed. Hence, special precaution has to be taken to make sure that the flesh should not become tainted or putrescent and that nothing impure be consumed with it. If such were the case, the entire procedure would prove abortive.

This at once explains three cardinal features of the Passover meal: the haste with which it had to be eaten; the unleavened bread; and the bitter herbs.

The meal had to be eaten in haste because otherwise the meat might become putrescent. For the same reason, what was not consumed had to be burned ere dawn.

Unleavened bread had to be eaten because leavened food is fermented, and fermentation implies putrescence. Had there been no such provision, the effect of eating the "pure" flesh would have been offset from the start.

The bitter herbs were a cathartic. They are invariably prescribed as such in the works of ancient physicians;

and the idea finds expression also in less "scientific" form in the widespread popular notion that they are a specific against demons or witchcraft. The ancient Greeks, for example, used to chew leaves of laurel and bay at their annual Feast of the Dead (Anthesteria) in order to prevent attack by ghosts; while their modern descendants eat garlic as a means of forfending pestilential spirits. The latter herb is likewise employed in the Balkans as a remedy against witchcraft and "the Evil Eye"; while in several parts of Europe, fillets of vervain are worn for the same purpose at such "witching seasons" as Midsummer Eve.

In the case of the paschal meal, the purpose of the bitter herbs was to neutralize any impurity which might accidentally have been consumed. Not improbably, however, ideas of magic may also have been introduced, and the herbs may well have served at the same time as a means of protection against those evil spirits which are everywhere believed to be especially rampant at the beginning of the year.

But, if Passover was a rite of family reunion, it was also automatically something more; for in primitive societies the family consists not only of its human members but also of its god. He too, therefore, was present at the meal, and he too was bound by the obligations of kinship which it imposed.

The idea that gods can be united to men by means of a sacramental meal is well attested in ancient religions. The Assyrians, for example, used to proffer an annual collation (*tâkultu*) at which the gods were invoked to bestow their bounty and protection; while a Canaanite document of the fourteenth century B.C. prescribes the placing of "seats" for the gods at a sacrificial ceremony Similarly, the Greeks held an "entertainment of the gods' (*theoxenia*) at Delphi in early spring; and in the Phrygian cult of the god Attis, "spreading a couch for the god" was a recognized synonym for "keeping the festival," couches being the customary seats at banquets. Lastly, in Exodus 18:12, the meal of reunion between Jethro, priest of Midian, and the Children of Israel is said, significantly, to have been eaten "in the presence of God."

The Passover feast of reunion was thus at the same time a guarantee of divine alliance and protection during the coming year.

But before the ceremony could be deemed effective, the ties of kinship which it established had to be made manifest by an outward sign; and, since the essence of kinship is blood, that sign had to be a sign of blood. Those who took part in the rite had to sign themselves with that common blood whereby their communion had been effected.

We have many examples, from both ancient and modern sources, of the custom of smearing sacramental blood upon the person. The practice of the Kumis of Southeast India has already been cited; and mention may be made also of the procedure in the Phrygian cult of Attis whereby initiants immersed themselves in the blood of a slaughtered bull. Nor, indeed, should we overlook the fact that it is this conception which ultimately underlies the Christian idea of being "washed in the blood of the Lamb" as the mark of communion and regeneration.

In the case of the paschal meal, however, what was involved was not so much the union of individuals with their families as of the families with the total clan or people. The signing had therefore to be done *upon their houses* rather than upon their bodies!

There are plenty of examples of this custom in modern times; and it is significant that in many of them the blood is sprinkled not on the houses of the human kinsmen but on that of the god or patron "saint," showing clearly that he too was treated as "one of the family"—the essential point of the entire procedure.

Thus, among the Amor Arabs, the blood of a sacrificial lamb is smeared on the lintel of the shrine of their patron sheikh. The same usage is reported also among the Druses of Lebanon and among the Kurds living near 'Ain Kalifê; while the Nosairis of North Syria sprinkle the blood of a slaughtered beast upon the door of the sanctuary of El Khidr (the Christian Saint George) so that "each household may enjoy good fortune during the year." So, too, at the New Year festival in Madagascar, a bullock is presented to the king and, after it has been slain, its blood is smeared with a wisp of grass upon doorposts and lintels. Finally, it may be observed that among many Arab tribes it is the custom to sprinkle blood upon any livestock captured in a foray, in order thereby to incorporate it with the tribal cattle.

Religious institutions rarely go back to one single motive. As a rule, they reflect a whole congress of thoughts, emotions, impressions, and insights, which fuse and blend not logically but naturally and which alternate, at different times and under different influences, as overtones and undertones of the resultant symphony. A given rite or practice may therefore possess more than one meaning or complexion, depending upon the particular prism through which it happens to be viewed.

This was especially true of the primitive seasonal rites which underlie the festival of Passover. Viewed from one angle, they were rites of communion—alike between man and man and between man and god. Their purpose was to establish ties of kinship, revitalize the family or clan, and, by the assurance of divine protection, promote the increase of livestock and crops for the coming year. Viewed

[2 1]

from another angle, however, these rites were an elaborate magical procedure designed to avert evil and misfortune.

From this second point of view, the family meal and the sprinkling of the blood were not so much ceremonies of communion as of *ransom*. The slaughtered beast was not an instrument of reinvigoration or a means of acquiring common blood and essence, but a surrogate for the people and their livestock as a whole. Similarly, the blood which was smeared on doorposts and lintels was not the token of common kindred but a piece of magical hocus-pocus guaranteed, for no ostensible reason, to forfend the assaults of affronted gods or malignant demons.

Under the influence of this idea, certain additional elements were introduced into the ritual. It was enjoined, for instance, that no bone of the slaughtered animal was to be broken. The reason for this was that the animal had come to serve as a symbol of the entire herd and as a propitiatory offering to the god. Accordingly (so it was believed), if it were maimed, a similar defect would befall the entire herd during the course of the year.

It was also under the impact of this idea that the primitive communal rite acquired its present name. Viewed as a magical procedure, its essential purpose was to ensure that gods and demons would *pass over* and spare the household or clan from hurt and harm. In the words of the Israelite saga: *When I see the blood, I will pass over you, and there shall no plague be upon you to destroy you* (Exodus 12:13).

CELEBRATION OF THE PASSOVER
(From the Schmid Haggadah, Venice, 1823)

In the foregoing pages we have sketched what is, on the whole, the most plausible and best-supported view of how the festival of Passover came into being. There is, however, an alternative view, and it is of such interest that it deserves at least to be stated.

This view starts from the fact that the Hebrew name for the festival, viz., *Pesach*, can also be derived from a word meaning "to limp," and that the performance of a limping dance happens to be a well-attested feature of religious rituals in both ancient and modern times.

Thus, when Elijah challenged the priests of Baal on Mount Carmel, the latter, we are told, limped beside the altar—the Hebrew word is *pasach*—as part of their statutory procedure (I Kings 18:26).

Similarly, Heliodorus, a Greek author of the early Christian era, informs us specifically that the seafaring men of Tyre, on the coast of Syria, used to worship their god by performing a strange dance, one movement of which consisted in *limping* along the ground.

Analogous performances are recorded also among the pre-Mohammedan Arabs and among the ancient inhabitants of both India and Ireland.

[23]

It is therefore contended by some scholars that, in origin, Pesach was a limping ceremony performed in connection with the primitive Palestinian spring festival.

But if so, what did the limping actually connote? Here, again, an alluring suggestion has been made.

The performance of a limping dance happens to be a characteristic feature of *mourning* ceremonies among Arab and Syrian peasants—so much so that in the Arabic and Syriac languages the word for *limp* comes to be a synonym for *mourn.* "It is customary," says the great Arabist Lane in his famous *Manners and Customs of the Modern Egyptians,* "for the female relatives and friends of a person deceased to meet together by his house on each of the first three days after his funeral, and there to perform a lamentation and a strange kind of dance. . . . Each dances with a slow movement and in an irregular manner; generally pacing about and *raising and depressing the body*" (italics mine).

Nor is this custom confined to modern times. An ancient Canaanite poem of the fourteenth century B.C. uses the word "hoppings" (or "skippings") in the sense of mourning exercises; and a Babylonian document now in the British Museum lists the term *hopper* (or *skipper*) as a synonym for *professional mourner.* Moreover, it is significant that the standard poetic meter used in ancient Hebrew dirges was distinguished by a special limping rhythm—a fact which would be readily explicable if they were designed to accompany a limping dance.

The limping, then, would have been a form of mourning exercise. But what, it will be asked, has this to do with a seasonal festival at the beginning of the year? The answer is arresting.

Ancient and primitive peoples often represent the cycle

of the seasons as the career of a god or spirit who dies annually during the dry and languid summer or during the bleak and barren winter but who is miraculously resurrected in the first flush of spring. The Egyptians had such a god in Osiris, the Babylonians in Tammuz, the Phrygians in Attis, the Syrians in Adonis, and the Greeks in Dionysus and Persephone. Each of these was believed to descend into the nether world, or otherwise vanish from the earth, during certain months of the year, to be eventually revived or retrieved amid great rejoicing.

Year by year, as the crucial season of harvest approached and men waited anxiously for the reëmergence of this beneficent spirit, they would bewail the fate that had overtaken him and cry upon his doom.

Sometimes, indeed, they would go even further and stage a mock funeral and resurrection. Plutarch tells us, for example, that as part of the Phrygian festival of Attis, in March, women used to bury a puppet and solemnly bewail it; while a similar custom is actually observed to this day before the autumn harvest festival by the peasants of Rumania.

At such a ceremony, the Limping Dance would have been peculiarly appropriate; and it is therefore suggested that the rite of Pesach, or Limping, originated in that practice.

On this theory, the basic ceremony from which the festival derived its name will have, of course, to be sharply distinguished from such other cardinal elements of it as the communal meal, the sprinkling of blood, and the eating of unleavened bread and bitter herbs. All that would be accounted for is the actual name Pesach.

3

ISRAEL IN EGYPT

*And it shall come to pass, when ye be come
to the land which the LORD will give you, according as he hath promised, that ye shall keep
this service.*

*And it shall come to pass, when your children shall say unto you, What mean ye by this
service? that ye shall say, It is the passover
[Pesach] sacrifice unto the LORD, who passed
over [pasach] the houses of the children of
Israel in Egypt, when he smote the Egyptians,
and delivered our houses. . . .*

*This is the night when the LORD kept
vigil, to bring them out from the land of
Egypt; This, then, shall be a night of vigil for
the LORD unto all the children of Israel
throughout their generations.*

Exodus 12:25-27, 42.

HOWEVER it may have begun, what Passover became in the tradition of the Israelites, and what
it has remained ever since, is a memorial of the
Exodus from Egypt.

The story of that event, as told in the Bible, runs as
follows. In a time of famine, a group of Hebrews known

as the Sons of Jacob came down from Canaan towards Egypt (Genesis 46:6-7). They settled, under a benevolent regime, in the Land of Goshen, and for some time thrived and prospered (Genesis 47:27). Later, however, when that generation had died out, a new king arose over Egypt who regarded their descendants as a potential "fifth column" in the event of war. He therefore reduced them to the status of slaves and set them to work building the cities of Pithom and Raamses (Exodus 1:6-11). When this king died, the oppression was continued and intensified by his successor (Exodus 2:23).

Eventually, a deliverer arose, named Moses. This Moses belonged to the priestly caste of levites, but he had been exposed in infancy in the rushes of the Nile and had been found there by the daughter of the Pharaoh, who had adopted him. One day, he saw an Egyptian belaboring a Hebrew, and therefore set upon him and killed him. Fearing a hue and cry, he then fled to Midian, where he married the daughter of a local shaman and tended the latter's sheep (Exodus 2:1-21).

While thus engaged, Moses happened on one occasion to come to a traditionally sacred mountain in the region of Horeb, and there beheld the curious spectacle of a bush wreathed in flames which seemed somehow not to consume it. Approaching nearer to this wondrous sight, he was vouchsafed a revelation by the local god Yahweh (Jehovah), who told him that He was none other than the ancestral deity of Israel under a new name, and that He would accomplish the release of the Israelites from Egypt and lead them to the paradisal land of "the Canaanite and the Hittite and the Amorite and the Perizzite and the Hivite and the Jebusite"—in other words, to what we now call Palestine and Syria. Moses was to introduce Yahweh to the Israelites and, after they had adopted Him, to go to Pharaoh and request the release of the people on the

[27]

grounds that they wished to keep a festival to that god at His sacred place (Exodus 3:1-8).

In order to authenticate that it was indeed Yahweh who had spoken to him, Moses was furnished with three magical credentials. First, his staff was turned into a serpent and then reverted to its normal shape. Second, when he placed his hand in his bosom, it became white, only to resume its natural color when he removed it. Third, he was told that if the people still persisted in questioning his mission, he was to give them visible proof of his authority by drawing water from the Nile and turning it to blood before their eyes. Moreover, he was instructed to retain possession of his staff, which would henceforth be endowed with magical powers (Exodus 4:1-17).

Thus commissioned, Moses repaired, with his brother Aaron, to the court of Pharaoh. Here another magical demonstration took place. Moses threw down his staff and it immediately turned into a serpent. The Egyptian magicians did likewise. But Moses' serpent consumed the rest (Exodus 7:10-12). Nevertheless, Pharaoh would not accede to his request.

Thereupon, the land of Egypt was visited by a succession of nine plagues, several of them induced by the lifting of Moses' magical staff. First, the rivers turned to blood. Then, in rapid succession, came visitations of frogs, lice, murrain, flies, boils, locusts, and darkness. Still Pharaoh was obdurate—until at last, on Passover night, Yahweh Himself came and slew the first-born of Egypt, passing over the homes of the Israelites, which He recognized by the ritual sign of blood smeared upon doorpost and lintel (Exodus 7:19, 12:51).

No sooner had the Israelites gone forth, however, than the Egyptians pursued them with a force of "six hundred chosen chariots and all the chariots of Egypt, and captains over all of them," catching up with them on the shores of a lake (called the Sea of Reeds) beside Pi-hahiroth, near Baal Zephon.

At this critical juncture, a divine miracle was wrought. An angel of God interposed a pillar of cloud between the Israelites and their pursuers, so that "one came not near the other all the night." Then Moses stretched out his hand over the lake, and God caused a strong east wind to sweep across it, dividing the waters so as to give passage to the Israelites. When, however, the Egyptians followed, the waters closed in upon them and they were drowned. "Thus Yahweh saved Israel that day out of the hand of the Egyptians . . . and the people believed in Yahweh and in his servant Moses" (Exodus 14:6-31).

A song of victory was then intoned (Exodus 15:1-21), and the long trek began towards the sacred mountain of God. Three months later, the caravan reached the place; and there a covenant was concluded between Yahweh and Israel. Henceforth, He was their national god, and they were His "peculiar people."

It is obvious to any unbiased reader that this story, with its markedly religious coloration and its emphasis on supernatural "signs and wonders," is more of a romantic saga or popular legend than an accurate record. Written down centuries later than the period which it describes, it is clearly more indebted to folklore than to sober fact.

The question therefore arises: Is it altogether fictitious? Is the whole story of Passover, as it is told in Jewish tradition, a mere figment of fancy—a pious invention? Or—if we ignore the legendary trimmings—is there independent evidence, outside of the Bible, for the sojourn of Israel in Egypt, its servitude under the Pharaohs, and its exodus therefrom?

The answer is that, while there is as yet no direct confirmation of details, and while neither sojourn nor exodus is in fact recorded in any known contemporary document, *the story as a whole*—apart, of course, from its purely miraculous elements—*is thoroughly consistent with all that we now know of the history of the Ancient Near East.*

That the presence of the Israelites in Egypt and their dramatic departure therefrom should not be mentioned in any extant Egyptian record is by no means so surprising as it seems. For the plain fact is that the Biblical account represents, after all, what is essentially no more than a family tradition. At the time when these events were supposed to have happened, the Israelites were not yet a nation, nor even a significant group. Therefore, while their fortunes and adventures might have been of the highest moment to their descendants and have served as a fitting subject for subsequent legend, they were not, at the time, of any particular interest to anyone else. To take a modern analogy: What happened to the Smiths or Joneses during the American Revolution might well be a sacred memory to their later generations and be preserved in family tradition with all sorts of pious and fantastic embellishments; but it is scarcely likely to find place in the formal records of the period!

Nor should it be objected that the drowning of the Pharaoh would have been an event of sufficient importance to be recorded, and that the absence of such a record, and the discovery of the relevant monarch's mummy, therefore discredit the Biblical account. For it is to be observed that, contrary to a prevailing impression, the Bible nowhere says that the Pharaoh was drowned. It speaks only of his "host" and "chariots" or of "the Egyptians" in general as having suffered this fate (Exodus 14:27-28, 15:4, 19), but not of the monarch himself, who may have directed operations from the rear and subsequently retreated. What is more, the statement (Exodus

14:6-8) that the Pharaoh himself participated in the pursuit may be but a figure of speech such as we use when we say that "the Government goes to war"; or it may be but a later legendary embellishment, born of a popular desire to enhance the victory of Israel and the miracle wrought by its god.

Viewed in the light of what is now known of Ancient Near Eastern history, the Biblical story takes us back to the troubled days of the early seventeenth century B.C., when hordes of Indo-Aryan invaders were sweeping across Asia Minor and Syria, carrying all before them. Many of the inhabitants of these areas, especially such as had been but resident aliens, took up their belongings and fled; until presently a vast, conglomerate army of displaced persons and refugees were to be found making their way southward through Canaan to the Land of the Nile.

Egypt had fallen, at the time, into weak hands. The administration was feeble and ineffective, and the incoming masses planned to take advantage of this situation. It was not long before their dream was fulfilled. In short order, they succeeded in gaining control of the country; and soon a new dynasty of kings—known to the Egyptians as the *Hyksos,* or Foreign Chiefs—were reigning in a new capital established at Avaris in the Nile Delta.

This political constellation proved especially propitious to a class of persons known as the *Hebrews.*

The term had no ethnic connotation. The Hebrews were not a distinct people, nor were they all of the same stock. They were simply the gypsies of the Ancient Near East—groups of nomads or seminomads who lived on the desert borders of the Fertile Crescent and who eked out a precarious living now as workmen in the urban communities, now as marauders, and now as mercenaries in the armies of rival sheikhs and emperors. They are mentioned

[3 1]

in ancient documents, from one end of the Near East to the other, throughout the entire period from 2000 until 1200 B.C. Nowhere do they appear to have enjoyed full civil status, and they are frequently styled "robbers" or "freebooters."

Whether these Hebrews formed part of the great Asiatic migration or whether they followed later and by stages, in the hope of settling peacefully under a sympathetic regime, is at present unknown. Certain it is, however, that some of them, too, began to move in the same direction; and it is among this group that the Bible includes the family of Jacob—a fact curiously illuminated by the occurrence of the name Jacob-her among those of known Hyksos princes.

The goal of the Hebrew immigrants, however, was not Egypt proper, but the Land of Goshen—a shallow valley, now known as Wadi Tumilat, which lies on the eastern border of that country and stretches, for some thirty to forty miles, from the Nile Delta to the region of Lake Timsah, in the Suez Canal Zone. Goshen had been a traditional pastureland for neighboring Asiatic bedouins; and here, in congenial surroundings, the Hebrews established their colony.

For several generations all went well. Then the wheel of fortune turned. Led by two spirited princes, the Egyptians rose against their Hyksos overlords and sent them fleeing into Canaan and Syria.

To the Hebrews living in Goshen these events may have caused alarm, but there was no immediate repercussion. The Hyksos capital was abandoned, and the court restored to the traditional site of Thebes, in the north. Nobody then bothered very much about a motley crowd of gypsies on a relatively distant reservation.

Eventually, however, things changed for the worse. The Egyptian Pharaoh Seti I (1318–1298 B.C.), return-

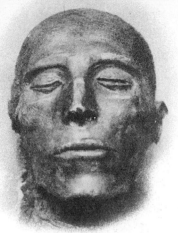
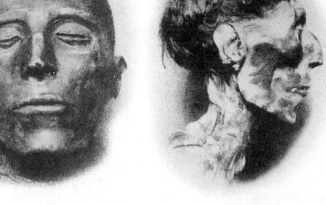

SETI I   RAMESSES II
The Pharaoh of the Oppression   The Pharaoh of the Exodus

ing from campaigns against the bedouins of Canaan, decided that his eastern frontier was dangerously exposed and that it would be prudent, for both military and political reasons, to move the seat of government back to the Delta and to rebuild Avaris.

When Seti died, his policies were continued by his son and successor Ramesses II (1298–1232 B.C.) The campaign against "the Asiatics" was pursued with relentless fury. At the same time, the renovation of the new capital was completed, and it was proudly renamed Per Ramesese, or "House of Ramesses"—the Raamses of the Bible. The monarch also engaged in other extensive building operations. Among them was the construction of a new store-city called Pi-Tum, "House of the god Tum"—the Pithom of the Bible—at a place in the Wadi Tumilat (Goshen), now marked by Tell Ertâbeh, near the fishing village of San el-Hagar.

These developments naturally brought the nearby He-

[33]

MEDIEVAL CONCEPTION OF PITHOM
AND RAAMSES
(*From the Prague Haggadah, 1527*)

brew colony strongly into the limelight. Ramesses came
to regard it as a potential "fifth column" made up of men
who were, in fact, kinsmen of the very foes whom he and
his father had been fighting and who might any day ally
themselves with them in a return attack upon Egypt. The
Hebrews were therefore reduced to the status of bond-
men, placed under the surveillance of commissars (the
"taskmasters" of the English Bible), and recruited for
forced labor on the new construction projects.

It was at this critical point, according to the Israelite
saga, that the deliverer Moses arose. Viewed in the light
of contemporary events, and without dogmatic precon-
ceptions, the genius and achievement of Moses would
seem to have lain in an inspired use of religion as a means
of freeing his people.

[34]

This, no doubt, was the result of his upbringing. Moses, says the tradition (Exodus 2:1-2), was a levite—that is, a member of the sacred caste which anciently served as acolytes at local shrines and to which, as is well known, a similar role was later assigned in the economy of Israel. Moreover, he was married to the daughter of a Midianite priest or shaman, and dwelt for some time in the latter's house (Exodus 2:21). It would therefore have been but natural for him to see the situation of his brethren through the prism of religious ideas.

Now, in ancient times, one of the most persistent of such ideas was that gods were strictly localized, being attached to specific places or communities, and that if you wanted to worship them, or establish relations with them, you had to go to the particular spots where they resided.

It was in this familiar idea that Moses saw the golden chance. If the traditional god of the Hebrews could be but identified with one who resided outside of Egypt, it might be possible to request permission, on a purely religious basis, to go out and hold festival to him—and then, of course, never come back!

The god whom Moses selected was JEHOVAH.* Hitherto, nothing whatsoever had been known about his origin, so that the reason for the choice and the implications of it have remained obscure. In recent months, however, a discovery has been made which puts the traditional tale in a new and arresting light.

On the walls of a temple built by Ramesses II—the Pharaoh of the Oppression—at Amarah West, in the

---

* The traditional form Jehovah is simply a mixture of the consonants of YAHWEH (JHVH)—the true name of Israel's god—and the vowels of the Hebrew word Adonai, "my Lord," which Jews reverently substitute for it in reading aloud. The form is here retained as being more familiar to English readers.

Northern Province of the Anglo-Egyptian Sudan, there has been found a list of African and Asiatic cities which that monarch claims to have captured. One ·of them is called, significantly, Jehovah-in-Edom. This means that Jehovah was, at the time, one of the recognized gods of that area. Now, Edom lies next door to Midian, where Moses lived and on the borders of which the revelation at the burning bush is said to have taken place. It is therefore not at all unreasonable to assume that Jehovah may also have been known in the latter region and that he may even have been the god of that Midianite cult in which Moses' father-in-law Jethro served as priest (see Exodus 3:1; 18:1-12).

In selecting this particular god, Moses was thus achieving two ends at the same time. First, he was giving the oppressed Hebrews of Goshen an opportunity to escape. Second, he was forging a religious basis for their affiliation with neighboring groups of ·the same type—a ·move which would obviously increase their chances of success in the task of conquest which lay ahead.

This second consideration seems, indeed, to have been the fundamental part of his plan. Moses must have known very well that, besides those who had settled in Goshen, there were many other Hebrews still roaming the deserts on the edges of the Fertile Crescent and that, for more than a century, these groups had been steadily penetrating into Canaan, threatening city after city and lending aid to the disaffected vassals of Egypt. (Warnings against their inroads bulk large in the famous Tell Amarna Letters, which contain the despatches addressed to the Pharaohs Amenhotep III and Amenhotep IV by their viceroys in Syrian and Palestinian cities.) It was to this more powerful movement that Moses planned to link his own band of exiles. What he envisaged was *a united Hebrew assault upon Canaan.* It was for this reason that

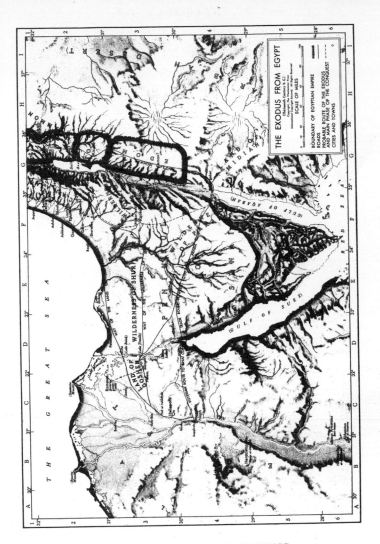

THE ROUTE OF THE EXODUS

he led his band thither; and it was for this reason also that he chose as the common god one who would be acceptable to the entire confederation and who was expressly described to Pharaoh as "the God of *the Hebrews*" (Exodus 5:3; cf. 3:18).

There were other groups also whom Moses would have wished to embrace in the movement; and this will explain why he caused his people to wander for long years around the peninsula of Sinai, instead of cutting straight across it, to their appointed goal.

The route which he chose led southward to a region of copper and turquoise mines; and from contemporary inscriptions found near some of them, at Serabit el-Khâdem, we now know that they were manned, at the time, by Semites from Canaan. Whether these were slave-laborers captured by the Pharaohs in their Asiatic campaigns, or whether they were professional smiths attracted to the spot in some ancient equivalent of a "gold rush," is as yet unknown; but in either case they would have constituted the kind of group with which Moses would have wanted to establish contact. There might, indeed, have been an even stronger reason. One of the clans of those Midianites among whom he had been raised, and in whose midst he had first conceived his plan, was called the Kenites, which means "smiths" (Numbers 10:29). It may therefore have been these people who were working the mines; and Moses would naturally have regarded them as certain allies.

In the mortuary chapel of Pharaoh Merneptah (1232-1224 B.C.) at Thebes there has been found a black granite stele, set up by that monarch in the fifth year of his reign, on which is engraved the record of his triumphs over various rebel peoples in the surrounding lands. Among his boasts occur the following significant words.

[38]

Israel is desolate; his seed is no more.
Palestine is become as a widow for Egypt.

This shows that the Israelites were already in Palestine by 1227 B.C. Allowing for the fact that the "forty years" which the Bible assigns to their wandering in the desert is but a round figure denoting a generation, and allowing also for the fact that the oppression must have taken place under Ramesses II (1298-1232), the principal rebuilder of Pithom and Raamses, *the Exodus will have occurred at approximately* 1250 B.C.

Thus, when the diverse strands are woven together, the Exodus of the Israelites from Egypt is seen to be but part of a larger historical tapestry, and what was previously but a blurred image stands out in bright and vivid hues. Romantic, fanciful, even fantastic as it may be, the traditional story of Passover is revealed, at the same time, as one of history's great epics of freedom.

4

FOLKLORE IN THE BIBLE STORY

WHEREVER the tale of the Liberation was told, teller and hearer alike loved to embroider its every detail and to weave around the record of fact the gossamer web of fancy.

The Biblical story itself is full of legendary traits.

1. Moses, the hero of the tale, possesses a wonder-working staff, endowed with all the properties commonly associated in popular lore with magic wands or saints' rods. It can assume the shape of a serpent, turn rivers into blood, bring on destructive plagues, divide streams, and produce water from rocks. This staff is the direct counterpart of the magical "pointing-stick" still used among the Blackfellows of Australia, and it is the prototype of what survives in degenerated form in the standard apparatus of the modern conjurer. More than this, it is but a milder equivalent of the wondrous weapons characteristically borne by the heroes of myth and romance—Indra's "whizzing bolt," Arthur's Excalibur, Siegfried's Balmung, and Odin's spear Gungnir. In the popular imagination, no hero could be without such equipment.

2. Before sending him on his mission, God supplies

Moses with three tokens of authority: his staff turns into a serpent and then resumes its normal shape; his hand becomes leprous and then recovers; and he converts water to blood (Exodus 4:1-9).

All of these signs recur elsewhere in the Biblical saga. When Moses and Aaron first appear before Pharaoh, Aaron casts forth his staff, and it turns into a serpent (Exodus 7:8-10). When Miriam, the sister of Moses, objects to his taking a Cushite wife, she becomes a leper, but is subsequently allowed to recover (Numbers 12:1-15). And when Moses wishes initially to demonstrate God's power to Pharaoh, he converts the rivers of Egypt to blood (Exodus 7:19-25). We may take it, therefore, that the three tokens of authority were drawn from the repertory of standard miracles familiar in the popular lore of the day.

But there is more to the matter than this. It is a common feature of folktales all over the world that a hero has to qualify for his mission by performing a set of seemingly impossible tasks. He has, for instance, to bring berries in winter, to wash black wool white, to skin a stone, to bind the waves of the sea, and so forth. It may therefore be suggested that it was a threefold test of this kind that popular imagination originally associated with the choice and appointment of the Israelite leader. Subsequently, however, the real point of the story came to be forgotten, and the miraculous feats performed by Moses were represented as tokens of authority graciously vouchsafed to him by God.

3. The host of Israel is said to be accompanied on its march out of Egypt by an "angel of the Lord" who goes before it (Exodus 14:19).

Here again we have an element of popular lore, for the belief in such a protective spirit is well attested among several ancient peoples. The Hittites, for instance, entertained the notion that armies were escorted by a god called Hasamilis who had the power of hiding warriors in moments of peril—an idea which finds its counterpart in the Biblical statement that, when the Egyptians were pressing hard upon them, the angel retired to the rear and interposed himself between the Israelites and their pursuers. Similarly, later Nabatean and Palmyrene inscriptions make mention of a god named Shiʻa Alqûm or "Accompanier of the Host," who escorted caravans.

4. The element of popular legend comes out especially in the story of the Crossing of the "Red Sea" (properly, the Sea of Reeds).

Moses has but to lift his magic staff over it, and immediately God sends a "strong east wind" which blows all night and causes the waters to divide (Exodus 14:16, 21-22).

As Sir James Frazer has pointed out, a very similar story is told among the African tribe of Wafipas. One of their kings, it is related, was once fleeing from his enemies when he found his path obstructed by the expanse of Lake Tanganyika. No sooner, however, had he sacrificed a sheep, dipped his staff in its blood, and struck the waters therewith than they immediately parted to afford him passage. (The point of the story is, of course, that by virtue of the sacral blood the staff acquires "divine" properties which compel the obedience of the waters.)

The story is also not without parallels elsewhere. Josephus and various Greek historians relate that when Alexander the Great marched against the Persian host of Darius, the Pamphylian Sea miraculously drew back and permitted his army to march through it. In a similar vein, too, the Roman historian Livy solemnly records that when Scipio the Elder was laying siege to the city of New

Carthage, during the Second Carthaginian War, the god Neptune suddenly came to his aid by causing the waters of an intervening canal to recede so that the invaders could cross it.

It is probable that in most of these instances, the legend of divine intervention clothes the memory of a remarkable natural phenomenon, for cases are indeed recorded of a sudden recession of waters due to the action of strong winds. In 1495, for example, and again in 1645, a strong wind drove back the waters of the Rhone into the Lake of Geneva for a distance of about a quarter of a league. "It looked," says the record, "like a wall of water [cf. Exodus 14:22!] . . . and the inhabitants could go down on dry ground between the bridges and pass from one bank to the other." So, too, in 1738, when the Russians were fighting the Turks, they were able to enter the Crimea at the Isthmus of Perekop because a strong wind suddenly blew upon the waters of the Putrid Sea, at the northwest corner of the Sea of Azov, causing them to recede and permit passage. It is recorded also by an eyewitness that, on one occasion, the waters of Lake Menzaleh at the entrance to the Suez Canal were driven back by the east wind as much as seven miles!

An incident of this kind would naturally form a ready theme for popular myth and legend.

5. It is possible also that the Israelites of a later age saw in this event at the "Red" Sea a reproduction in history of one of the most familiar of ancient Oriental myths.

All over the Near East the story was told of how, in the gray dawn of the world, certain rebellious powers had conspired against the supreme Lord, or against the Master of the Earth, and how he had done battle with them and defeated them and (according to several ver-

[43]

sions) despatched them into the nether world or drowned them in the sea. After this triumph, said the story, the victorious god had built himself a palace on his holy hill, or repaired to one of his established centers, and there installed himself as king, to receive the adoration of his heavenly and earthly subjects.

The myth is found among Egyptians, Babylonians, Hittites, and Canaanites alike; and there are parallels to it in the literature of India, Greece, and the ancient Teutons.

Now, according to the Bible, when Moses and the Children of Israel saw the Egyptians discomfited in the waters of the "Red" Sea, they broke out into a kind of paean celebrating that triumph. The words of their song are given in the fifteenth chapter of the Book of Exodus.

Scholars have long recognized that, to speak in relative terms, the song is "modern"—that is, the product of a far later age. It was used in the same way as popular snatches are used in many an ancient chronicle—as an interlude to break the monotony of the prose recital. But when we study its wording carefully, a curious fact emerges. The historical victory which it is supposed to celebrate is described in terms peculiarly appropriate to the old mythological combat. The foes of Jehovah sink into the sea; the nether world engulfs them (verses 5, 10-11). The god blows upon them with his wind (verse 10), just as in the Babylonian myth the victorious Marduk drives the storm-wind into the belly of his adversary Tiamat. By virtue of his triumph, he leads his people to "the mountain of his inheritance," where his sanctuary is upreared and he is acknowledged as king forever (verses 17-18). In precisely the same way, the Babylonian god establishes a palace for himself and is hailed as sovereign lord; and in the same way, too, in the Canaanite version of the tale, the god Baal follows his defeat of the monster

Yam ("Sea") by repairing to the "hill of his inheritance" and there installing himself as everlasting king.

It would appear, therefore, that the writer of this song consciously assimilated the victory at the "Red" Sea to the triumph of the divine champion in the time-honored myth. The drowning of the Egyptian host recalled that of the primeval rebels; the launching of the "strong east wind" immediately brought to mind the device which the god had employed in worsting those upstarts; the leading forth of Israel to the sacred mountain of Horeb provided the same sequel as was to be found in the ancient myth, when the god betook himself to the "hill of his inheritance" whereon he was installed in state. Once again, popular fancy clothed the facts of history with the glamorous raiment of legend.

5

PASSOVER LEGENDS OF THE JEWS

All who enlarge upon the story of the Going Forth from Egypt shall be deemed praiseworthy.

IT WAS not only the Biblical writers who invested the historical record with fanciful traits. As the story passed from father to son, later generations attempted to read new meanings into the old words and to wrest from them a deeper, universal significance.

The fruits of these efforts are scattered throughout the pages of subsequent Hebrew literature, and they have become part and parcel of traditional Passover lore. They possess, of course, no sort of dogmatic authority, and no one is obliged to accept them as anything more than quaint tales and whimsical conceits. Their purpose is solely edification. By skillful manipulation of the plain literal sense and by ingenious combination with other passages of Scripture, almost every word and phrase of the sacred text is made to carry a richer import and, where occasion demands, a legend is promptly invented to support it. No detail is too small for notice, none too trivial for elaboration.

The scripture says, for example, that the lives of the children of Israel were embittered "with hard service, in mortar and in brick" (Exodus 1:14). To the rabbis, the mention of the two materials had to carry a special meaning. Every day, they explained, the cruel Egyptians imposed upon the Israelites a set quota of bricks to be laid, and for every brick short of that amount they took an Israelite child and sealed it up alive in the very building in which its parents were toiling. In this way, the lives of God's people were literally made bitter "through mortar and brick"!

Again, if the scriptures said that Moses served as a shepherd and drove his flock through the wilderness (Exodus 3:1), for the children of a later age the words held a deeper import. Moses, they said, had served as a shepherd in order to learn how to lead God's flock, and his days had been passed in the wilderness because it was there that Israel was destined to wander for forty years and because it was thence that, in the end of days, Moses would again lead the redeemed into the presence of God.

Nor was it allowed to pass without comment that God had revealed Himself in a lowly bush of thorns rather than from a tall cedar or the peak of a lofty hill. All of this was symbolic. Garden hedges are made of thorns, and God wished thereby to show that Israel was to be the hedge of the world, which is His garden. Moreover, as the thornbush cannot live without water, so Israel cannot live without the "living waters" of the Word of God, and as the thornbush bears roses as well as thorns, so Israel, be its estate never so lowly, would also be adorned by the fragrance of the pious.

The rod with which Moses performed "signs and wonders" was no ordinary rod. It was cut from the Tree of Life, or, according to an alternative tradition, hewn from the sapphire of the divine throne. It had been created in the twilight of the first Sabbath eve, and had been handed by God to Adam. From Adam it had passed to Enoch,

[47]

thence to Noah, from Noah to Shem, from Shem to Abraham, from Abraham to Isaac, from Isaac to Jacob, and from Jacob to Joseph. On the latter's death, it had been stolen by the Egyptians and placed in Pharaoh's palace. But Jethro, the father-in-law of Moses, had removed it and planted it in his own garden. There it served as a test for the suitors of Jethro's daughter. Like Excalibur, the sword of King Arthur, none could pluck it up save only the appointed hero. And that hero was Moses.

MOSES WIELDS THE MAGIC ROD
(*From the Prague Haggadah, 1527*)

On the rod were inscribed the Ineffable Name of God and the initials of the ten plagues. And it is this rod which the Messiah will bear in his hand.

When, in obedience to the revelation at the burning bush, Moses returned from Midian to Egypt, his mount was no ordinary beast. Moses rode on the same ass as Abraham had saddled on that eventful morn when he had "risen up early" to obey the will of God and sacrifice his only son on the top of Mount Moriah (Genesis 22:3). Moreover, it was this same beast, said the rabbis, that would ultimately bear the Messiah to Zion when he came, as the prophet had foretold, "lowly and riding upon an ass" (Zechariah 9:9).

[48]

Nor did popular imagination fail to elaborate the incidence of the plagues. These, said the legend, lasted altogether for one year, because that is the length of time appointed by God for a man to pay the penalty of his sins. The Flood likewise lasted a year, and so too did the affliction of Job.

It was not by chance that the first plague was the turning of the Nile into blood. The Egyptians regarded that river as a god; and the Holy One, blessed be He, thought that if they but saw him discomfited, this would be sufficient by itself to turn them from their evil ways.

When the fourth plague befell them, the Egyptians tried to keep the wild beasts from their houses by barring the doors. But God was not to be foiled, so He promptly created a special termite to bore through the woodwork.

It was not in blind fury that God slew the first-born of Egypt. This was in requital of the fact that an Israelite woman had been forced to miscarry her child while treading mortar for Pharaoh. But the angel Gabriel had taken the infant's body, molded a brick around it, and carried it up to heaven. That brick is the footstool of God.

The prescribed ritual of the Passover likewise lent itself readily to fanciful interpretations.

The reason why a lamb was chosen as the sacrificial beast was that the Egyptians worshipped the ram, and the children of Israel had to show publicly that they disavowed such idolatry before God would release them from bondage.

The blood smeared on the sideposts of the door and on the lintel of every Israelite dwelling was a reminder of the three patriarchs, Abraham, Isaac, and Jacob; while the bunch of lowly hyssop with which it was applied symbolized the House of Israel—lowly, yet bound together by the grace of God.

Especially did the fancy of later generations dwell on the Crossing of the "Red" Sea.

Why, it was asked, did Moses have to lift his rod over it in order to make it divide? Because, came the answer, when, on the instructions of God, he first commanded it to do so, the Sea refused to obey on the grounds that it was older than man and would not take orders from him. Moses reported this refusal to God. "What," said God, "does a master do when his servant disobeys him?" "He beats him with a rod," replied Moses. "Very well," said God, "go thou and do likewise!"

Before its waters had parted, the Israelites, confident in the protection of God, had been quite willing to jump into the Sea and swim or wade across it; and the various tribes had even quarreled with one another for the honor of entering it first. Benjamin, the youngest of them, took matters into his own hands and jumped in. This so enraged Judah that her princes started to pelt the Benjaminites with stones. God, impressed by the devotion of both tribes, decided to reward them. Jerusalem, the abode of His presence, was therefore located in the territory of Benjamin, while the royalty of Israel was conferred upon Judah.

Pharaoh was not drowned. At the end of fifty days, God hauled him out of the "Red" Sea. He will never die, but stands forever at the gate of Hell to proclaim to all earthly monarchs who pass through it that there is indeed no god like the Lord.

When Israel saw the Egyptians drowned in the Sea while they themselves had passed through it dry-shod, they came at last to a full and confident belief in God and in His servant Moses. It was only by the power of this belief that they were able to sing the great Song of Triumph; for faith is a necessary condition of praise. That is why it is first written, *And they believed in the Lord*

[5 0]

and in His servant Moses, and only thereafter, *Then sang Moses and the children of Israel* (Exodus 14:31, 15:1).

Even the angels, who had hymns of praise upon their lips, were silenced until this song was over. And in the world to come, when all generations pass before God and ask Him which shall be first to recite His praise, the choice will fall upon those who went with Moses through the Red Sea; and they will sing the same song once more.

6

THE SEDER

THE CENTRAL and most familiar feature of Passover today is the Seder—that is, the service held in the home on the first two nights of the festival. This now takes the place of the sacrifice and paschal meal.

Before the festival begins, all leavened food (such as bread, flour, beer, and the like) is carefully removed from the household. At nightfall on the preceding evening, the master of the house makes a thorough search of the premises, using a candle to light up hidden nooks and corners. Whatever leavened food he finds is put aside until morning and then burned. The search is introduced by a blessing and concluded by the pronouncement of a formula in the Aramaic language declaring that "all leaven, whether detected or undetected, is hereby regarded as nonexistent or as mere dust of the earth."

In common practice today, the ceremony is performed symbolically. The mistress of the house previously undertakes an elaborate "spring cleaning," even substituting special crockery and silverware for that used during the rest of the year. A few crumbs of bread are then left deliberately on the floor for the master of the house to "discover" and remove. He sweeps them with a feather into a wooden spoon which he then binds with a handkerchief or rag. In the morning, the spoon and its contents are burned.

Should the eve of Passover fall on the Sabbath, all leaven except that required for the Sabbath meals is "searched" on Thursday night and burned on Friday morning.

In the evening, at dusk, the mistress of the house lights the two candles which mark both the Sabbath and every Jewish festival, and the Seder table is laid. The following articles must be placed upon it:

1. *Three cakes of unleavened bread (matzah)*, one above the other. These are usually baked especially thick, and are known as *Mitzvoth* or "Commandments," i.e., cakes reserved for ritual use. The top one is popularly known as "the Cohen," the second as "the Levite," and the third as "the Israelite."

2. *Bitter Herbs* (e.g., horseradish), commemorating

THE REMOVAL OF LEAVEN
(From a prayer book, Amsterdam, 1870)

[53]

those which the Israelites were commanded to eat along with the paschal lamb (Exodus 12:8). Nowadays they are taken to symbolize the bitterness which the Egyptians inflicted upon the children of Israel (Exodus 1:14).

3. *Haroseth*—a mixture of chopped apple, nuts, raisins, and cinnamon, pounded into a kind of paste. The real purpose of this is simply to allay the sharpness of the bitter herbs, but it is popularly interpreted as symbolizing the mortar which the Israelites were forced to tread during their bondage in Egypt.

4. *A Roasted Egg,* commemorating the special additional sacrifice offered in the Temple on Passover. (It is interesting to observe that the Passover egg survives also in popular Christian usage, for one of the most familiar of Easter customs is that of painting special eggs, originally called Pasche eggs. They are taken to be symbolic of regenerated life and thence of the Resurrection.)

5. *The Shankbone of a Lamb*—a symbol of the paschal sacrifice.

6. *Parsley or radishes*—the characteristic "side-dishes" of an ancient banquet.

These articles are arranged in a special order upon a large dish placed in front of the master of the house. The cakes of unleavened bread, covered with a cloth, occupy the center. Above them, to the right is placed the shankbone, and to the left the roasted egg. Below them, to the right are the bitter herbs, and to the left is the *haroseth*.

In addition, sufficient wine must be provided to fill four cups for each member of the company. The drinking of these, at stated intervals, is obligatory. Various reasons are given. According to some, the four cups correspond to the four expressions used in Exodus 6:6-7 to describe God's deliverance of Israel from Egypt, viz., "*I will bring you out* from under the burden of the Egyptians, and *I will rid you* of their bondage, and *I will redeem you* . . .

and *I will take you to Me for a people.*" Others assert, however, that the cups have reference to four passages in Scripture in which it is declared that, in days to come, the wicked will be made to drink from the cup of God's wrath; while yet a third explanation insists that they allude, on the contrary, to four passages which mention the cup of comfort and salvation proffered by God unto the faithful.

It should be added that in some communities, e.g., among the Jews of Yemen, five cups are drunk, and that earlier usage seems to have confined the number to three.

Lastly, in the center of the table, a large goblet is set for the prophet Elijah, who is believed to come as a guest to every Seder meal—a precursor of the Messiah.

It is customary throughout the Seder to adopt a leaning posture, instead of sitting upright. This commemorates the ancient fashion of reclining at meals and is also re- garded as symbolic of the ease and freedom which Israel came to enjoy as the result of its liberation from Egypt.

The master of the house sits at the head of the table, propped up on cushions. In many parts, he wears a long white cloak known as a *kittel*. This cloak is also worn on New Year and the Day of Atonement; and it is in this garment—a symbol of purity—that a man is both married and buried.

The essence of the Seder is the recital, with appropriate hymns and prayers, of the story of the Going Forth from Egypt. The narrative—called the Haggadah—is based on the account of that event given in Scripture, interspersed with rabbinic comments and elaborations. In the form in which it has come down to us, it is not the work of any one man or the product of any one period, but represents a gradual growth. Some of the basic elements are prescribed already in one of the treatises of the Mishnah and date, in their recorded form, as early as the third century A.D.,

CELEBRATION OF THE SEDER
(*From a manuscript Haggadah, 1738*)

though even then they rest upon a yet more ancient tradition, ascending to the time of the Second Temple. Other elements, however, are of far later origin. Some of the songs, for instance, which are today appended to the main body of the service originated only in the fifteenth century. Moreover, these later elements are by no means standardized, but vary from place to place in accordance with local usage and tradition.

The service begins with the sanctification (*Kiddush*)—the traditional inauguration of sabbaths and festivals in Jewish homes. The first cup of wine is poured, and the master of the house pronounces a blessing, in which all join, thanking God especially for the Festival of Unleavened Bread, "the season of our liberation."

After the wine has been drunk, the celebrant washes his hands and distributes parsley dipped in salt-water to every member of the company. Eaten after the pronouncement of an appropriate blessing, this serves as a kind of *hors d'œuvres*.

The celebrant next takes the middle cake of the unleavened bread and breaks it in half, wrapping one of the halves in a napkin and laying it aside for use at a later stage of the proceedings. The other half is then exhibited to the company and the celebrant explains that it represents *the bread of affliction which our forefathers ate in the land of Egypt*. With this he couples an open invitation to *all who are hungry* to *come and eat* and to *all who are needy to come and celebrate the Passover feast*, adding that *though this year we be here, next year may we be in the land of Israel; though this year we be slaves, next year may we be free men!*

The formula is recited not in Hebrew but in Aramaic, because that was the vernacular of the Jews at the time when it was composed. Legend says, however, that the reason why the more exotic language is used is that otherwise evil spirits might accept the open invitation. These spirits know Hebrew, but they do not understand Aramaic!

The second cup of wine is now filled, and the youngest person present asks four questions, the answers to which constitute the body of the Haggadah.

Why, he asks, *is this night different from all other nights? For on all other nights we eat leaven and un-leavened alike, but on this night only unleavened. On all other nights we eat any kind of herbs, but on this night only bitter herbs. On all other nights we do not dip even once, but on this night twice. On all other nights we eat either upright or leaning, but on this night we all lean!*

The framing of these initial questions has been modified in the course of the ages. Originally, there were only *three* of them, and the third inquired pertinently: *Why is it that on other nights we can eat meat boiled, roasted or stewed, but on this night only roasted?* The question referred, of course, to the prescribed manner of preparing the paschal lamb (Exodus 12:9). When, however, the Temple was destroyed and sacrifices ceased, it clearly lost all meaning and was therefore dropped. Conversely, the fourth question, relating to the custom of leaning at meals, was a later addition, because the Jews learned this custom only when they came into contact with the Romans. The question relating to the twofold "dipping," it should be added, is altogether obscure and it is significant that no answer is, in fact, given to it! In all probability, it refers to some feature of the earlier ceremony which later fell into disuse.

With the answer to these questions the Narrative proper begins.

Quoting Scripture (Deuteronomy 6:21), the celebrant replies that *We were slaves unto Pharaoh in Egypt, and would still be so, had not the LORD our God brought us*

out thence with a strong hand and an outstretched arm.
Accordingly, he adds, *even if all of us were scholars, well versed in the Law, we would still be obliged to recount the tale, and every embellishment of it deserves praise.*

There follow some rabbinic comments, of uncertain origin, relating to the recitation of the Haggadah at night. Then comes the section of the Four Sons.

THE FOUR SONS
(From the Schmid Haggadah, Vienna, 1823)

Four times in the Bible is mention made of "thy son's" inquiring about the meaning of Passover. But each time the question is framed in a different manner. Once (Deuteronomy 6:20), he is made to ask: "What are these testimonies and statutes and judgments which the LORD our God has commanded us?" This, say the rabbis, is the question of a wise son. A second time (Exodus 12:26), however, the question runs: "What means this service *of yours?*" This, say the rabbis, is the question of a wicked son, for he excludes himself. A third time (Exodus 13:14), the inquirer asks simply: "What is this?" This, say the rabbis, is the question of a simple son. The fourth time (Exodus 13:8), the question is asked only by implication;

the Israelite is instructed to "tell thy son." This, say the rabbis, refers to the son who is too young to ask.

Each is to be answered in kind. The wise son is to be instructed in all the minutiae of the ritual, and the father is to take care to tell him that "in accordance with the customary laws of the festival, people are not expected to go gadding around to parties after the meal is over!"

The wicked son is to be told bluntly that, since he now excludes himself from the observances of Israel, had he been living at the time he would likewise have been excluded when it was brought out of Egypt!

The simple son is to be told simply that *by strength of hand the LORD brought us out of Egypt, out of the house of bondage.* He will not understand subtleties.

As for the one who is too young to ask, he is to have the ceremony explained to him on a purely *personal* basis: *It is because the LORD did something for me when I came out of Egypt.* He will not appreciate historical lessons or national implications.

The Section of the Four Sons is followed by a few passages of rabbinic discussion relating to the precise date of the ceremony. Then the narrative begins anew: *In the beginning our forefathers worshipped idols, but the Almighty brought us near to His service.* This was originally an alternative beginning of the Haggadah. Two forms have now been blended together.

The celebrant then lifts the cup of wine and pronounces the words which today form the leitmotif of the entire Seder: *God's promise it is that has stood by our fathers and us. For it is not one alone that has risen up to destroy us. In every generation men rise up to destroy us, but the Holy One, blessed be He, delivers us out of their hand!*

The story of the Sojourn in Egypt and the Deliverance is thereupon related in summary form, each successive episode being illustrated by an appropriate biblical quota-

tion and expanded by fanciful rabbinic comment. Israel
went down to Egypt *and sojourned there:* that means that
he was but a transient, not destined to settle. He went
down few in number (Deuteronomy 10:22)—but now he
is as numerous as the stars. *The Egyptians treated him ill
and afflicted him and imposed hard service upon him,* but
he cried to the Lord, and his God heard him *and looked
on his affliction and ill treatment and oppression, and
brought him out with a strong hand and an outstretched
arm, with great terribleness and with signs and wonders*
(Deuteronomy 26:8).

No angel or seraph was it that wrought this deliverance,
but *the Holy One, blessed be He, by His own glory and
by His own Self. For is it not written: I will pass over the
land of Egypt in this night, and I will smite the first-born
in the Land of Egypt . . . and execute judgments
against all the gods of Egypt—even I, Jehovah myself*
(Exodus 12:12)?

And what was this "mighty hand," this "outstretched
arm," this "great terribleness," these "signs and wonders"?
By dexterous manipulation of the sacred text, the rabbis
found the answer.

The "mighty hand" was the plague of murrain, because
in telling of it the Scripture says: "The hand of the Lord
fell upon the cattle" (Exodus 9:3).

The "outstretched arm" was the sword of God; for is it
not written that David saw the angel of God "poised between heaven and earth, with a drawn sword in his outstretched hand" (I Chronicles 21:16)?

The "great terribleness" was the revelation of God's
presence; for the Bible says distinctly: "Hath ever a god
assayed to go and take him one nation from the midst of
another by trials and signs and wonders, by war and by a
mighty hand and an outstretched arm and by great ter-
riblenesses, even as all which the LORD your God did

for you in Egypt before your eyes" (Deuteronomy 4:34).

The "signs" were the magic rod of Moses, for by that rod were they wrought (Exodus 4:17).

And the "wonders" are the plague of blood; for it is written in the Book of Joel the prophet (2:30): "Wonders in heaven and earth—even blood and fire and pillars of smoke."

There follow some intricate and ingenious disquisitions about the exact number of the plagues. When the latter are enumerated, it is customary to dip the finger into the winecup and sprinkle a few drops. This is a relic of the ancient custom of pouring libations to forfend evil spirits. It is felt that the very mention of the plagues must be accompanied by this protective measure!

The narrative proceeds with what may be termed the Litany of Wonders—a cumulative poem reciting the successive benefits conferred by God upon Israel. Each line ends in the ringing refrain *Dayyenū*, "Alone 'twould have sufficed us!" chanted as a response by the company. The following extracts will illustrate the general scheme of the poem:

> *If He had cleft the Sea for us,*
> *nor let us pass dryshod,*
> *DAYYENŪ!*
> *If He had let us pass dryshod,*
> *nor sunk our foes therein,*
> *DAYYENŪ!*
>
> . . . .
>
> *If He had led us to the Mount,*
> *nor given us the Law,*
> *DAYYENŪ!*
> *If He had given us the Law,*
> *nor brought us to the Land,*
> *DAYYENŪ!*

If He had brought us to the Land,
nor built His Temple there,
DAYYENŪ!

The poem speaks of *fifteen* such beneficent acts, and the sages were not slow to seize upon the fact. Fifteen, they explained, is the numerical value of the Hebrew letters Y and H which together spell *Yah*—one of the names of God, and fifteen were the steps leading to the Holy of Holies!

After the telling of the story comes the explanation of the ritual—a portion of the Haggadah which is quoted already in the Talmud.

The celebrant points to the shankbone (taking care not to lift it up) and quotes the Biblical verses relating to the paschal lamb.

Then he lifts up the unleavened bread and again quotes the appropriate verse (Exodus 12:29).

Finally, he displays the bitter herbs. These, he explains, symbolize the bitterness wherewith the Egyptians afflicted the lives of the children of Israel (Exodus 1:14).

But mere explanation is not enough. The ritual contains a message; and this is now brought home in words which have become immortal wherever Jews are foregathered:

> *Every man in every generation is bound to look*
> *upon himself as if he personally had gone forth*
> *from Egypt. . . . It is not only our fathers that*
> *the Holy One redeemed, but ourselves also did*
> *He redeem with them. For does not the Scrip-*
> *ture say: And He brought* us *out thence that*
> *He might bring* us *in, to give* us *the land which*
> *He swore unto our fathers* (Deuteronomy
> 6:23)?

[63]

The winecup is then raised and, after a short introduction, the recital of the Hallel begins. The word Hallel means "Praise," and it denotes the group of Psalms, 113-118, which form a statutory part of the liturgy on new moons and festivals. (These, it may be observed, are the "songs of praise" which Jesus and the disciples are said to have sung at the Last Supper—itself the paschal meal.) The Hallel is peculiarly appropriate to the Passover festival because Psalm 114 (*When Israel went forth out of Egypt*) describes events connected with the Exodus.

The second cup is then drunk. All present wash their hands.

The celebrant breaks the topmost cake of the unleavened bread and that half of the middle cake which he did not previously lay aside, and gives thereof to each person, together with a small portion of horseradish. This, he explains, commemorates the practice of the great Rabbi Hillel (fl. 30 B.C.-9 A.D.), who insisted that such a "sandwich" should be eaten in order to fulfill to the letter the Biblical command to eat bitter herbs and unleavened bread *together* (Exodus 12:8)!

The evening meal is then served, a favorite preliminary dish being hard-boiled eggs dipped in salted water. After the meal, the celebrant unwraps the reserved half of the middle cake and everyone receives two pieces, called *afikoman*. This is usually interpreted as the Greek *epikōmion,* or "dessert." Actually, this is an error. The Mishnah says: *Men should not leave the meal to go revelling,* using the Greek word *epikomioi.* This was mistakenly rendered: *Men should not omit* afikoman *after the meal.* The word was then taken to denote the concluding consumption of matzah!

Two quaint customs attend the distribution of the *afikoman.* The first is that children are permitted to hide the reserved portion of unleavened bread and claim a ransom for it before delivering it up to their fathers. The service cannot proceed without it. The second custom is to preserve one of the two pieces of the *afikoman,* either in a sachet or by inserting it between the pages of the prayer-book, as a charm against evil spirits!

After grace has been said, the third cup is drunk. The "goblet of Elijah" is then filled, and the main house door is flung open while the following words are recited:

> *Pour out Thy wrath upon the heathen that know Thee not and upon the kingdoms that call not on Thy name; for they have devoured Jacob and laid waste his habitation* (Psalm 79:6). *Pour out upon them Thy fury, and let the heat of Thine anger overtake them* (Psalm 69:24). *Pursue them in anger, and destroy them from under the heavens of the LORD* (Lamentations 3:66).

Why these verses should have been associated with the proffering of a goblet to Elijah is a point which did not escape the ingenuity of the rabbis. Passover, it was explained, is expressly described in the Bible (Exodus 12:42) as "a night of watchings" (in the plural)*; and one of these "watchings" is for Elijah, the precursor of the Messiah. The goblet proffered to him, however, is not merely a token of welcome; it is a symbol of the "cup of reeling" which he will give the heathen to drink, and also of the "cup of comfort" which will be quaffed by Israel. Elijah, it is added, must surely come on Passover night, because is not that the night of redemption?

A favorite Jewish belief is that Elijah *does* come year by year and sip the goblet, although no diminution of its contents is apparent. It is also a prevalent superstition that

---

* This is a literal rendering of the Hebrew text. The English Bible translates: "a night . . . much to be observed."

if an unmarried male visitor should happen to enter while the door is open "for Elijah," he will marry a daughter of the house.

In the Middle Ages, the opening of the door served a more dramatic purpose. Since Passover very often coincided with Easter, Jews were especially exposed at this season to the infamous libel that they used Christian blood for ritual purposes. The door was therefore flung open so that all might behold the complete innocence of the proceedings. It is believed by some that the accompanying execration was directed especially against those who spread the dreadful slander and perpetrated the massacres to which it gave rise. The rabbis, however, were careful to point out that it referred only to those who, in historical fact, had destroyed the Temple in Jerusalem, and that all who worshipped the one God were exempt from its terms.

The chanting of the Hallel is now resumed, followed by miscellaneous hymns.

At its conclusion, a doxology is recited, and the fourth and last cup of wine is drunk.

A benediction over the wine follows, and this is caught up in turn by the intonation of verses from an eleventh-century poem originally designed for the Sabbath of the Passover week. The poem declares that the prescribed ritual has now been carried out in all its detail, and offers a prayer that those who have partaken in it may be spared to do so again in the coming year:

> *O Thou, exalted in Thy purity,*
> *Gather them that number'd ne'er shall be!*
> *Emplant the saplings of Thy vine again!*
> *To Zion lead Thou back this captive train!*

This completes the formal portion of the Seder.

7

SONGS OF THE SEDER

THE FORMAL PORTION of the Seder is followed, in popular custom, by the chanting of hymns and folksongs. These vary from place to place. In Western countries, however, a number of them have become more or less standardized, and now form an integral element of the proceedings.

The first of these, recited only on the opening evening, rehearses, in an alphabetical acrostic, a series of miracles which are said in the Bible to have been performed, like that of the Passover, in the dead of night.

> *Laban the Syrian didst Thou affright,*
> *Lord, in the dead and darkness of the night;*
> *And Israel wrestl'd with an angel's might;*
> > *And 'twas the dead of night.*

> *Daniel, who read the visions of the night,*
> *Sprang from the lion's den; the Agagite,*
> *Dread Haman seal'd our ruin and our plight;*
> > *And 'twas the dead of night.*

> *O haste the day which is nor day nor night!*
> *Make known, O Lord, that Thine is day and night!*
> *Set watchmen o'er Thy city day and night!*

Make bright as morn the darkness of our night!
For now 'tis dead of night.

The authorship of this poem, which had been part of the Haggadah for centuries, was unknown until, some thirty years ago, the late Professor Israel Davidson made the romantic discovery that an ancient manuscript of the Greek Bible which had been engaging the attention of scholars was actually written over a yet older Hebrew document. This turned out to be a copy of the poems of Yannai, a Jewish liturgist of the seventh century, and one of those poems was our hymn! Originally composed for the Sabbath in the Passover week, it was later transferred to the Haggadah.

On the second night of the festival, a similar poem by the famous liturgical poet Eleazar Kalir (fl. seventh century) is substituted. This rehearses, again in an alphabetical acrostic, all the events which are believed in Jewish legend to have taken place at Passover—e.g., the visit of the angels to Abraham, the destruction of the evil city of Sodom, the fall of Jericho, and the hanging of Haman. At the end of each verse runs the refrain:

> *So might ye say:*
> That *was then the paschal sacrifice!*

Of a quite different order is the poem *Kî lô nā'eh*. Of unknown authorship, this poem—again an alphabetical acrostic—recites the various attributes of God:

> *Awful in sovranty,*
> *Beyond equality,*
> *Cohorts of His recite:*
> > *To Thee and to Thee,*
> > *Thine, for 'tis Thine,*

[68]

> Thine is the Kingdom,
> Thine, also Thine!
> God it befits,
> Him it beseems!

It is probable that the quaint refrain of this poem is really but a series of catchwords referring to Biblical verses which were intended to be sung in full. Thus, the words *To thee and to Thee* would seem to refer to Psalm 65:2: *To Thee* is praise beseeming, O God, in Zion, *and to Thee* should vows be paid. Similarly, the words *Thine, for 'tis Thine* would be an allusion to I Chronicles 29:11: *Thine, O LORD, is the greatness, and the power, and the glory, and the victory, and the majesty . . . for Thine* is all that is in heaven and earth. Lastly, the words *Thine, also Thine* would refer to Psalm 74:16: *Thine* is the day, the night *also is Thine*; or perhaps to Psalm 89:11: *Thine is* the heaven, the earth *also is Thine*.

The hymn *Addir Hū* has, perhaps, the most rousing tune in the entire Seder service, and it is the one in which the company usually joins with the greatest gusto. Dating, in all likelihood, from the fifteenth century, it was long current in Germany as a concluding melody for the service; and an ancient Yiddish version of it, sung to the same melody, is still popular. In the ritual of the Jews of Avignon (France), this poem was sung as a general festival hymn, by no means reserved for Passover. Once more, it is an alphabetical acrostic enumerating the attributes of God and imploring Him to

> *build, God,*
> *build, God,*
> *build Thy House right soon!*

It is curious to note that the very same attributes as

are here assigned to God are likewise assigned—in the same alphabetical order—to his honor the bridegroom in a modern Jewish wedding-song from Yemen!

Following these more religious hymns come two pure folksongs, both probably originating no earlier than the fifteenth century. The first is a counting song:

> *Who knows one?*
> *I know one.*
> *One is our God in heaven and on earth.*
> *Who knows two?*
> *I know two.*
> *Two are the Tables of the Covenant,*
> *One is our God, etc.*
> *Who knows three?*
> *I know three.*
> *Three are the patriarchs, etc.*

WHO KNOWS THREE?
The Three Patriarchs
Abraham, Isaac, and Jacob

WHO KNOWS FOUR?
The Four Matriarchs
Sarah, Rebekah, Leah, and Rachel

(From a manuscript Haggadah, 1738)

Who knows four?
I know four.
Four are the matriarchs, etc.
Who knows five?
I know five.
Five are the Five Books of Moses, etc.

The count proceeds to thirteen (*the thirteen attributes of God;* cf. Exodus 34:6-7), and this has led to the suggestion that the song was originally designed as a kind of catechism for boys, an additional verse being learned each year until they reached the age of thirteen and attained religious majority.

The song has counterparts, of course, in all languages, the most familiar in English being the well-known

Who'll tell me one—O?
I'll tell you one—O.
One is God and all alone and evermore shall be so.

The last song of the Haggadah is the most familiar. This is the famous *Had Gadyâ* ("Only One Kid"). Written in doggerel Aramaic, it is a cumulative song of the same type as *The House That Jack Built* or *The Pig Who Wouldn't Get over the Stile,* and is believed to be an imitation of a fifteenth-century German rhyme entitled *Der Herr der schickt den Jockel aus* ("The Master who sent the yokel on an errand"). The song relates the chain of events which followed when a little kid "bought by my father for a couple of coins" was set upon by a fox. The fox was bitten by a dog, the dog was beaten by a stick, the stick burnt by fire, the fire quenched by water, the water drunk by an ox, the ox slaughtered by a butcher, the butcher slain by the angel of death and—in a breathless and inspired climax to the entire Haggadah—the angel of death by the Holy One, blessed be He.

The song was popularly interpreted as an allegorical history of Israel. The kid was Israel, purchased by God for the price of the two tables of the Covenant. The fox was Assyria, the dog Babylon, the stick Persia, the fire Greece, the water Rome, the ox the Saracens, the butcher the Crusaders; and the angel of death the Turkish domination.

Both the *Had Gadyâ* and the preceding song were at first unknown to the ritual of the Spanish and Portuguese (Sephardic) Jews, since they were of German origin. They first appear in print in an edition of the Hagadah published at Prague in 1590. Today, however, they have become familiar to Jews in all countries.

THEN CAME THE HOLY ONE, BLESSED BE HE,
AND SLEW THE ANGEL OF DEATH
(*From a manuscript Haggadah, 1738*)

8

MORE PASSOVER SONGS

BESIDES those which have acquired more general use and thus become part and parcel of the Haggadah, there are many Passover songs of more limited distribution, preserved only by one or other community. These are to be found in local prayer-books or in editions of the Haggadah printed in out-of-the-way places. The Library of Congress in Washington, D.C. possesses a special collection of such more exotic publications.

The songs are usually composed in Hebrew, but by no means always. Because of their essentially popular character, they are often written in the vernacular rather than in the sacred tongue. The vernacular of Jews in Eastern Europe was Yiddish—a mixture of Hebrew and German; while that of the Spanish and Portuguese Jews was Ladino or Spaniole—a similar mixture of Hebrew and Spanish.

The following song is taken from the so-called *Mahzor Romania,* printed at Venice in 1524. It is sung after the drinking of the fourth cup of wine, and is based upon the rabbinic dictum that all which happened in Egypt on the night of Israel's liberation will be repeated at the final redemption of the Jews from their exile. In the Hebrew original, the contrast is pointed up by defining the present oppressors of Israel as "Edom"—a term frequently used in the later literature to avoid dangerous mention of actual names:

The marvels, Lord, which Thou didst erst display
In Egypt, do again this sorry day!

In Egypt didst Thou signs and wonders send;
So let the clouds of smoke again ascend,
And let the foeman see his bitter end!

In Egypt, o'er the rooftops, in the night,
Didst Thou pass over. Now, O Lord, alight
To dwell in majesty on Zion's height!

In Egypt, on a fleeting cloud didst ride
Of old, O Lord. Now, once again, bestride
That cloud, and visit all the sons of pride!

In Egypt, Israel murmured as a bride:
"The bridegroom cometh." Now, let it be cried
From rooftops: "Comes thy Champion to thy side!"

Moses and Aaron didst Thou send of old
In Egypt. Now, Messiah to Thy fold
Send thou in triumph and in glory stol'd!

O Thou Who in the lofty height dost dwell,
In Egypt didst Thou save us. Now, as well,
Save us from tyrant and from infidel! *

And here are verses from a poem found in the prayer-book of the Jews of Carpentras, eloquent of the sadness

---

* In the original: *Deliver us from Rome and Ishmael*—a reference to the oppression which the Jews suffered from the Church and from Islam.

[74]

which so often clouded the celebration of the festival in
medieval times:

> In Egypt, when they held the feast
>   They were redeem'd and free;
> But we who keep it here, O Lord,
>   Are bow'd 'neath tyranny.
>
> In Egypt, when they held the feast,
>   Thy hand was bared to save;
> But we—we cower and we cringe
>   Beneath Thy fury's wave.
>
> In Egypt, when they held the feast,
>   Her firstborn didst Thou slay;
> But now it is my sons, O Lord,
>   That they would sore assay!
>
> In Egypt, when they held the feast,
>   Each household slew its sheep;
> Now—on the Lamb of Israel
>   The desert jackals leap.
>
> .   .   .   .
>
> Tho' bread unleaven'd was their food,
>   And bitter herbs their fare;
> Thou freed'st them, Lord. So unto us
>   Our liberty declare!

Another song from Carpentras, current also in Avignon, play especially on the Song of Songs which, as we
shall see, is "recommended reading" for the festival. Israel,
the beloved of God, is bidden hie away from her exile and
return to Zion; and there is a constant contrast between
the lands of the Dispersion and the sacred soil:

.   .   .   .

From where diviners scan the skies
    And would all secrets know,
Rise up, my love, and come away
    To where the brooklets flow.

.   .   .   .

From where men every lie contrive,
    And live on loot and spoil,
Rise up, my love, and come away,
    To Gilead's fair soil.

.   .   .   .

From where the only thing men seek
    Is rash iniquity,
Rise up, my love, and come away
    To where God seeks for thee.

.   .   .   .

From where a shadow as of death
    Falls on thy neighbor's door,
Rise up, my love, and come away,
    To where men want no more.

.   .   .   .

From where no seed is sown nor reaped
    Save violence and lust,
Rise up, my love, and come away
    To lands of corn and must.

.   .   .   .

From where thick darkness fences in,
    And where deep shadows hem,
Rise up, my love, and come away;
    Next year in Jerusalem!

9

THE SAMARITAN PASSOVER

THERE is one part of the world in which the ancient Paschal Sacrifice is still performed as in Biblical times. At Nablus, site of the ancient city of Shechem in Palestine, lives the fast-dwindling community of the Samaritans. Reduced to no more than two hundred souls, the Samaritans claim that they are the surviving remnant of the House of Israel, the descendants of men who were never carried into captivity but remained always on their ancestral soil. They reject every part of the Bible except the Five Books of Moses, and they claim that the appointed place of God is not Zion (as the Jews maintain) but Mount Gerizim, at the foot of which they reside. Here, according to their tradition, the patriarchs are buried and it was here too that Abraham prepared to sacrifice his only son Isaac.

The Samaritans live under the governance of a high priest and in strict conformity with the Mosaic law. They believe, however, that, in consequence of sin and transgression, they are at present passing through a period of divine displeasure, marked by the withdrawal of God's presence and the suspension of the sacrificial system. The only sacrifice which they still offer is that of the Passover. The rite is performed on the slopes of Mount Gerizim, the entire community repairing thither and spending the week under canvas.

The following account of the ceremony is translated from a voluminous work on Samaritan beliefs and practices compiled, toward the end of the nineteenth century, by the then high priest, Jacob ben Aaron (1840–1918). The work, which is entitled *The Guide* (*Dalíl*) and which still exists only in manuscript form, is drawn from older sources, and is therefore obviously more reliable and authoritative than the many journalistic descriptions with which curious tourists and ill-informed spectators have flooded the popular prints during recent years.

"When the fourteenth day of the first (lunar) month approaches, they all get ready and foregather at the Chosen Place, at the spot selected on the soil of the Mountain for the performance of the sacrifice. Men and women alike foregather, and each pitches his tent with great rejoicing and gladness of heart. On the fourteenth day itself, they remove all yeast from their places, and wash all the vessels. They also wash their clothes and change their garments. They refrain from all leaven and ban it from their midst. On that day, they eat no bread whatsoever, be it leavened or unleavened, in accordance with a tradition passed down from antiquity concerning the observance of this institution. The tradition is based on the commandment of Exodus 23:18: 'Thou shalt not sacrifice over leaven the blood of My sacrifice.' The Samaritans, then, are forbidden to keep possession of anything fermenting into yeast on the fourteenth day of the month.

"If, in any given year, the day of the Paschal Sacrifice— that is, the fifteenth day of the month—falls on a Sabbath, the ceremony has to take place on the Friday, after sunset. The leaven has therefore to be removed during the course of the day itself, so that the consumption of the Paschal meal shall be free of contamination therefrom, i.e., so that there shall not be in their stomachs any matter which is fermenting into leaven.

"At the beginning of the tenth hour, the high priest goes to the place where they have the oven, accompanied by the elders of the community and the slaughterers, and together they light the fire in it. The oven is dug out in the ground, after the manner of a well, and is lined with stones, put together without mortar. It is three cubits deep from the ground-surface, but its length and width depend on the number of sheep to be sacrificed. One of the elders stands by until the flame catches, and the stones glow. At half past the tenth hour, the altar itself is lighted. On it they lay wood, for the burning of the fat. In the middle they place copper vessels to boil water for the removal of the fleece from the sacrificial sheep, together with the ashes, the sheep itself being destined later to have its flesh torn in pieces by human hands. The fire is kept burning under three vessels.

"Half an hour before sunset, the members of the community present themselves amid great rejoicing and pomp. Those of the elders who are advanced in years dress in beautiful clothes, entirely white. Then they all foregather in a large cluster beside the altar on which the sacrifice is to be offered, standing in rows on its south side; the priest especially appointed for the task stands in front of them. Lads and young children come too, all clad in linen coats and linen breeches and wearing linen girdles and linen caps. All stand around the altar, those who are to do the slaughtering taking up a position at the very edge of it. Each of these holds in his hand a sharp, flawless knife. Then the priest proceeds to inspect the lambs which they have prepared for the sacrifice, removing those in which a blemish is detected. Thereafter, the lads take them and round them up, and place them in front of the altar, themselves standing all round them. Some twenty minutes or a quarter of an hour before sunset, the priest begins to intone hymns appropriate to the praise of God, and he seeks Divine pardon for sin, and acceptance of the offering. All this is recited in the holy tongue, Hebrew.

SAMARITANS SLAUGHTERING THE PASCHAL LAMB

"The priest next begins a short prayer for the slaughtering. Thereafter he continues in Hebrew: *For I call on the name of the Lord; ascribe ye greatness unto our God, The Rock,—His work is perfect, for all His ways are justice; a God of faithfulness and without perversity, righteous and upright is He* (Deuteronomy 32, 3-4). *Blessed be our God forever, and blessed be His name forever!* Then he reads a portion of that section of the Law in which the LORD has commanded Israel to offer the Paschal Sacri-

[8 0]

fice (Exodus, 12). When he reaches the words: *And all the congregation of the community of Israel shall slaughter it at twilight*, the slaughterers proceed to slay the sheep quickly, in accordance with the prescribed regulations, sprinkling its blood on the altar round about, and all saying in a loud voice: *They proclaim and say, There is no God but one!* This they repeat three times. Then they add: *The LORD, a God gracious and merciful, long-suffering and abundant in loving-kindness and truth* (Exodus 34:6).

"The slaughtering takes place at twilight. The rules by which eventide is determined among the Samaritans are as follows: The first stage is from the moment when the sun grows red until the moment it begins visibly to set. The second is from the moment it begins visibly to set until it is altogether obscured. This lasts about an hour and a half. Real twilight is the space of two minutes after the actual going-down of the sun. This is the moment when the Paschal Sacrifice is slaughtered.

"When the slaughtering is finished, the people exchange greetings. First, they kiss the hand of the High Priest and of all the men of his family, and later pass to the other members of the congregation, starting with the eldest and ending with the youngest. The men who stand around the altar then proceed to pluck the hair from the sacrificial victims, loading the animals upon the shoulders of the serving-lads, and removing the stomach, dung, fat, kidneys, and midrift, which they place above the wood on the altar, sprinkling the whole with salt and washing them clean of all impurity. Then they cut deep gashes into the lambs and remove the ischiac nerve, concerning which it is said in the Torah: *Therefore the Children of Israel eat not the ischiac nerve unto this day* (Genesis 32:33). They also drain off the blood, applying liberal applications of salt. No bone is allowed to be broken, in accord-

[81]

ance with the commandment of Exodus 12:9. The whole body of the lamb is placed on wooden spits, head downward. While all this is being done, part of the bystanders recite from the Torah, beginning at Exodus 12:1 and ending at the conclusion of Chapter 15. They accompany the reading with hymns and praises, and add also several other verses from the Torah in which mention is made of the Paschal Sacrifice. Meanwhile, the priest takes unleavened bread, together with bitter herbs, and gives to each to eat.

"When they have finished preparing the lambs, they take them and lower them by the spits into the midst of the oven, which faces the altar on its eastern side. Over the top of the oven they place a wooden trellis, covering it with greenstuff and applying to the top of it a paste of mud, which they plaster firmly over it to prevent the smell from coming through. All the while, they sing and intone hymns to God. The flesh is then left in the oven for three hours, during which they recite the Evening Prayer handed down from remote antiquity. The fire is left burning on the altar until no fragment of the fat or legs is left. It is "a pleasant savour unto the LORD."

"When night has fallen and the Evening Prayer has been concluded, they come and remove the sacrificial meat from the oven. At that juncture, they have their loins girded, sandals on their feet, and staves in their hands, as ordained in Exodus 12:11. Each lamb is then taken apart, and when all have been thus dismembered, the congregation begins to recite hymns to a pleasing tune. These are composed in Aramaic and are the work of ancient sages. After this, the priest recites the words: *Blessed art Thou, O LORD, our God. There is no God but one, and His is the greatness. May our festive season be happy, through God's grace!* Then they sit down to eat of the Paschal Sacrifice, doing so in haste. Each family eats sep-

arately, men and women apart. With the meat they par-
take of wafers of unleavened bread, together with bitter
herbs.

"None of the meat is removed from the place where
they happen to be encamped. When they have finished
eating of the sacrifice, they gather all the remnants and
burn them on the altar.

"That same night, when dawn breaks, they rise up and
recite the Morning Prayer. This continues until two hours
after sunrise. When it is over, each man returns to his
tent in joy and in gladness of heart.

"Such then is the institution of the Paschal offering
among the Samaritans. It should be added that if there be
any internal blemish in the lamb, or if it be maimed or
scarred, it is removed to a place apart. It is not eaten nor
merely thrown away, but burnt separately. It may not be
given to a Gentile to eat. It should also be observed that
during the time in which the Sacrifice is being prepared,
no Gentile may come into contact with a Samaritan, nor
may anyone eat of the sacrifice or even approach it if he
be in a state of ritual uncleanness.

"Whatever is found next morning lying over on the
ground is gathered up and burnt on the altar."

10

DEW

Passover marks the beginning of the season when, in Palestine, the heavy showers of the winter months are replaced by the light rains of spring. On the first day of the festival, therefore, special prayers for these "dews" are inserted in the morning service of the synagogue. During their recital, the cantor customarily attires himself in a white robe—usually the *kittel*, of which mention has already been made (p. 55).

The prayers consist mainly of liturgical poems in which Israel is represented as the bride of God awaiting the bestowal of His grace. A fine specimen of this type is a song by the great Spanish Jewish poet Solomon ibn Gabirol (1021–1058), which forms part of the Sephardic or Spanish and Portuguese rite. As is common in medieval Hebrew verse, it contains an acrostic on the author's name, which is preserved in the following translation:

> *Seared, O Lord, is Thy beloved's face;*
> *On her dear face the sun of Egypt burns.*
> *Let then Thy dewdrops fall upon her face,*
> *On her dear face which unto Thee she turns.*
>
> *Most gentle Lord, when men cry bitterly,*
> *Only from Thee comes forth their answer true;*
> *   Shield of them who put their trust in Thee,*
> *Now answer her with Thy refreshing dew!*

Sometimes, however, themes of deeper import are introduced. Thus, another poem by the same writer, likewise included in the Sephardic liturgy, plays on the verse of Isaiah (26:19) in which it is said that *Thy dead shall live; my dead bodies shall arise. Awake and sing, ye that dwell in the dust; for thy dew is a shimmering dew, and the earth shall cast forth the shades.* The following translation, which again preserves the acrostic, will perhaps convey its general spirit:

Send, Lord, Thy gentle wind, and let it blow
On all our dead, and let Thy dew descend
Lightly upon them, that they wake and know,
O Lord, that with Thy dawn their sleep hath end.

Most gentle Lord, Who art so good to all,
Only from Thee is our delivering;
None but Thyself can free us from his thrall
　　And turn Death's winter to eternal spring.

Yet another Sephardic hymn, sung to a rousing melody, plays on the prophecy of Hosea (14:5) in which God is made to declare: *I will be as the dew unto Israel: he shall blossom as the lily, and cast forth his roots as a tree of Lebanon.* This poem lacks the sublimity of those already quoted, and the general "feel" of it may best be represented by a doggerel paraphrase:

Welcome, O dewfall;
　Rainfall, adieu!
Great in salvation,
　God sends the dew!

My songs will I sing,
　My rhymes will I rhyme;

To God my Salvation
Rise they sublime!

Now shall my verses
Distil as the dew.
Great in salvation,
God sends the dew.

This is Thy glory,
This is Thy fame:
Israel, Thy people,
Is called by Thy name.
Grant it salvation;
Send Michaël;
Loud let him cry it,
Loud let him tell:
"I come as the dewfall
To thee, Israël!"

Finally, the blessing of spring rain is invoked in an alphabetical acrostic of rare ingenuity if also of somewhat banal taste:

Our God and the God of our fathers,
A-glistening with dewdrops
Render the earth!
Blessed with dewdrops,
Render the earth!
Cheerful with dewdrops
Render the earth!
Drench'd with rich dewdrops
Render the earth!
Effulgent with dewdrops
Render the earth! . . .

[86]

THE SONG OF SONGS

The Bible contains in its collection of "holy writings" five small books known in Jewish tradition as The Scrolls. They are: the Book of Ruth, The Song of Songs, Ecclesiastes, Lamentations, and Esther.

One of these Scrolls is "assigned reading" for each of five important dates in the Jewish year. Ruth, with its background of the gleaning, is read on the second day of Pentecost, the festival of the spring harvest; while Ecclesiastes is reserved for the third day of the Feast of Booths. Similarly, Lamentations forms part of the liturgy for the Ninth of Ab when, according to tradition, both the First and the Second Temples were destroyed; and Esther is intoned publicly on the Feast of Purim, whose story it relates. The prescribed book for the eighth day of Passover is The Song of Songs.

In early times people wondered at the inclusion of an apparently secular work in a collection of books supposedly sacred in character. It was not difficult, however, to find an explanation. The song was interpreted as being allegorical. No earthly love of man and woman did it celebrate, but the passion of a Divine Lover for his beloved people Israel. The maiden who was "my dove, my perfect one" was the maiden Israel, and the lover who was "conspicuous among ten thousand" was Israel's God.

Every verse was thus interpreted in symbolic and mystic fashion, and almost every verse lent itself readily to this procedure. What pious homilies could be woven out of such simple words as "I was asleep, but my heart waked. Hark! my beloved knocked, saying, Open to me, my sister, my love, my dove, my undefiled" (5:2)! And with what exquisite, if bizarre, fancy could the breasts of the beloved which "are like two fawns, the twins of a roe" (4:5) be taken to symbolize Moses and Aaron!

This method of interpretation was taken over by the Christian Church, which made of the Song a celebration of the mystical love between Christ and His Church. It is this interpretation that you find in the chapter headings of the King James Version, though they have been omitted from more modern renderings.

From the earliest times, however, there were scholars who were content to take the song as it is, and who regarded the celebration of human love as sufficiently holy to warrant the inclusion of the Song among the "Holy Writings." Said Rabbi Akiba, in the first century: "Since all of the 'holy writings' are holy, the Song of Songs is the holy of holies"; while, four hundred years later, the celebrated Church Father Theodore of Mopsuestia even exposed himself to anathematization for maintaining that the book was to be understood in a literal sense. Similarly, in the twelfth century, the famous Jewish commentator Abraham ibn Ezra produced an explanation of it on purely secular lines; and it is this method of interpretation which today holds the field.

Yet what are we to make of the actual song? Is it a unity, or is it a collection of short madrigals and ditties? The answer depends upon the meaning we attach to the title "Song of Songs." There are some who say that this is a pure Hebrew superlative like "slave of slaves," "king of kings," or "holy of holies." It would then mean simply "the choicest of all songs." There are others, however, who say that the title means "a song made up of songs," and that it is essentially an anthology.

Late in the eighteenth century the German poet Herder came up with a peculiar theory to account for the assumed unity of the song. It was suggested that it was in reality a pastoral drama. A girl from the village of Shunem (i.e., the Shulamite) had been abducted by the king for his harem in Jerusalem. Her lover, a peasant lad, visited her, "peered through the lattice," and sang his love for her. Such verses as "the king hath brought me into his chambers, yet will we rejoice and be glad in thee" were taken to support this view.

The foundation, however, is flimsy, for the crucial verses can be otherwise interpreted. Thus, the lines just cited can be translated equally well: "Were even the king to lead me to his chambers, still would we be glad and rejoice in thee." Apart from this, it must be remarked that this kind of drama does not elsewhere appear in the whole range of ancient Semitic literature, and that it is consequently very doubtful whether such a form of composition was indeed known to the early Hebrews.

Others, again, have suggested that our book was derived ultimately from Babylonian chants recited in the worship of the divine lovers Ishtar and Tammuz. That an analogous cult actually existed in Syria is well known from the myth of Aphrodite (Astarte) and Adonis. The parallels which have been adduced, however, between the wording of the Song and that of the ritual chants are scarcely convincing; and it must be remembered, in any case, that the language of love is bound to be much the same whether it be expressed in a secular ode or a religious hymn.

Another explanation of the Song was put forward

some fifty years ago as the consequence of observations made by the Consul Wetzstein among the Syrian peasantry. Wetzstein noticed that Syrian wedding festivities lasted for seven days, and that during these seven days the bride and the bridegroom were enthroned as king and queen, and dances were held before them. Then the queen would dance a sword-dance before her bridegroom, the while he praised her bodily charms. The same sort of festivity, it may be added, obtains to this day among the Jews of Yemen.

On the basis of these observations it was held that The Song of Songs was a collection of wedding-songs sung in similar circumstances. The long descriptions of bodily charms would then fall into place, while the reference to the king and to Solomon would be complimentary allusions to the bridegroom. Verses like the following would be descriptions of the bridegroom's procession:

> *What is this that cometh up from*
> *   the desert, like pillars of smoke,*
> *Scented with myrrh and frank-*
> *   incense, with all the powders of*
> *   the merchant?*
> *Behold, it is Solomon's couch,*
> *   Threescore warriors are around it,*
> *Chosen from the warriors of Israel*
> *   They are all of them girt with the sword,*
> *Skilled in the waging of war;*
> *   Each hath his sword on his thigh,*
> *For fear of alarum by night.* (3:6-8)

The reference to the bride as a "Shulamite" would also be a compliment. "Shulamite" would be an alternative pronunciation of "Shunemite," and the point of the compliment would be to liken the bride to Abishag, the

Shunemite beauty who comforted King David in his old age. Again, the difficult lines, "What see ye in the Shulamite? As it were the dance of two camps [Mahanaim]" (6:13) would be an illusion to the customary sword-dance!

It must be admitted that this theory is not unattractive, but a detailed comparison of the Syrian songs—*wasfs*, as they are called—with the Hebrew text does not really bear it out. It would be safer to say only that certain parts of the song may have been taken from wedding-ditties wherein bride and groom were likened to a king and queen. To go further than this is to abandon caution for speculation.

Lastly—saving the best till the end—there is the purely natural interpretation of the Song as a collection of songs. The repetitions which occur in it do not militate against this view. A snatch of song, once it has become popular, is often caught up in divers compositions. You get similar repetitions in Homer, which is certainly not a unity.

On this view, The Song of Songs would be a *corpus* of Palestinian love-songs. They need not have been written in any one single place or at any one single date. As a matter of fact, compositions very similar to The Song of Songs, and often employing the same metaphors, are found in ancient Egyptian lyrics ranging in date from 2000 to 1100 B.C. Moreover, by dint of repetition, it is possible that the original wording often got distorted and changed, so that we cannot argue from the linguistic peculiarities of the present Hebrew text the original date of composition.

Certainly, as the text now stands, the language would seem to indicate that in all its parts it is later than the time of King Solomon, to whom the ancient editors of the Bible ascribed it. The Hebrew is of a much later type than was common in the Solomonic period, and scholars have even recognized in it words borrowed from Persian and Greek. But even if its present form is comparatively late, the songs out of which our book is composed may well have been traditional and therefore of far higher antiquity. Allowance must be made for continual adaptation and modernization in the mouths of succeeding generations, as also for dialectic variations and peculiarities.

EPILOGUE

I T is not by accident that the festival which commemorates Israel's release from bondage also commemorates the beginning of its new trials in the wilderness. This, perhaps, is the real message of Passover. When a people has ceased to be enslaved and is prepared to brave disaster in the search for Revelation—then indeed the season of its freedom is at hand.

Judaism does not believe in a passive freedom but in an active redemption. A man is not free simply because he is not a slave. A man is free when he assumes responsibility for himself and when he fights for that self-realization which is the true revelation.

Yet freedom is not mere independence, nor liberty mere license. Freedom, says the Passover message, is redemption through God. It is not because they went out of Egypt that Israel became a free people; it is because they set their faces towards Sinai.

This message is as immediate today as it ever has been in the past. It is important to remind ourselves that freedom is not to be won by the easy road of escape, but that it implies an active and combatant struggle for the realization of spiritual ideals and the mobilization of spiritual consciousness.

The answer to slavery is not absence of slavery, but

militant struggle for independence. Men must be prepared to fight for their freedom without compromise and without capitulation. They must look not backward to Egypt but forward to the Promised Land, and they must be prepared to wander for forty years in order to reach it.

It is not only the joy of deliverance that the Passover festival recalls, but also the pain. Its message is that there are no half measures. *Not by the hand of an angel, and not by the hand of a seraph, and not by the hand of any one man sent, but by His own glory and by His own self did the Holy One, blessed be He, bring us forth out of Egypt.*

BIBLIOGRAPHY

THE LITERATURE about Passover is immense, and only a few titles can be mentioned here. Those who wish to inquire further into some of the topics discussed in this volume will find much of interest in the following works.

THE BIBLICAL PASSOVER: G. B. Gray, *Sacrifice in the Old Testament* (1925), pp. 337-82; J. Morgenstern, "The Origin of the Massoth and the Massoth-Festival," in *American Journal of Theology*, vol. xxi, pp. 274-93.

PASSOVER IN TEMPLE TIMES: The ceremonies are described in the Mishnaic treatise Pesahim, which may be read in H. Danby's translation. A popular account is: H. Schauss, *The Jewish Festivals* (1938), 48-55.

ORIGINS OF PASSOVER: The significance of eating and drinking together as a means of establishing kinship is discussed by Wm. Robertson Smith, *The Religion of the Semites* (3rd ed., 1927), ch. viii; see also E. Crawley, *The Mystic Rose* (3rd ed., 1927), ch. vii.

Analogies to the smearing of blood on the doorposts and lintels are described by S. I. Curtiss, *Primitive Semitic Religion Today* (1902), ch. xv, and by Crawley, *op. cit.*, vol. i, pp. 290-99.

On the magical use of bitter herbs, see: A. Lods, *Israël* (1938), p. 340; H. Friend, *Flowers and Folk-Lore* (1886), pp. 171, 547; J. G. Frazer, *The Fasti of Ovid* (1929), vol. ii, pp. 160 ff.

[95]

On the significance of keeping the paschal animal intact, see: K. Kohler, "Verbot des Knochengebrechens," in *Archiv fuer Religionswissenschaft,* 1910, pp. 153 ff.

On rites of limping, see: W. O. E. Oesterley, *The Sacred Dance* (1923), p. 117 ff.; A. J. Wensinck, *Some Semitic Rites of Mourning and Religion* (1917), p. 43; Stanley A. Cook, in Robertson Smith, *op. cit.,* p. 671.

ISRAEL IN EGYPT: G. E. Wright, "Epic of Conquest," in *The Biblical Archaeologist,* vol. iii (1940), No. 3; Jack Finegan, *Light from the Ancient Past* (1946), pp. 103 ff.; T. J. Meek, *Hebrew Origins* (1936), pp. 32 ff.

The "Israel Stele" of Pharaoh Merneptah is translated in Finegan, *op. cit.,* p. 105.

On Jehovah-in-Edom, see: H. W. Fairman, "The Four Ages of Amarah West," in *The Illustrated London News,* April 17, 1948.

Extracts from the Tell Amarna Letters relating to the Hebrews (Habiru) are translated conveniently in S. A. B. Mercer, *Extra-Biblical Sources for Hebrew and Jewish History* (1913), pp. 9-20.

FOLKLORE IN THE BIBLE STORY: On tests given to heroes, see the examples cited in Stith Thompson, *Motif-Index of Folk Literature* (1934), vol. iii, pp. 320 ff.

On parallels to the Crossing of the Red Sea, see: J. G. Frazer, *Folk-lore in the Old Testament* (1918), vol. ii, pp. 456 ff. On the possible basis of this event in natural phenomena, see: Naville, *Journal of the Victoria Institute,* vol. xxvi (1893), pp. 27-29; Tulloch, *ibid.,* vol. xxviii (1896), pp. 267-68.

PASSOVER LEGENDS OF THE JEWS: Later Jewish legends about the Sojourn and the Exodus are collected in Louis Ginzberg's classic *The Legends of the Jews* (1909 ff.), vol. ii, pp. 245-375; vol. iii, pp. 5-36—a work to which the present writer acknowledges his indebtedness.

SEDER AND HAGGADAH: The best editions of the Haggadah in English are those by Cecil Roth (1934) and by David and Tamar de Sola Pool. There is also an attractive edition, with verse translations, by Maurice Myers and another by Maurice Samuel. The Jewish Reconstruction Foundation has produced a "revamped" version of the traditional service, with several innovations, in its *New Haggadah* (1942); while Reform Judaism has its own *Union Haggadah*. The most convenient critical edition is that produced by E. D. Goldschmidt for the Schocken series (1937). This is unexcelled. The leading rabbinical commentaries are collected and reprinted in J. D. Eisenstein's *Hagadah* (1920), an encyclopaedic work from the strictly Orthodox viewpoint.

An extremely interesting discussion of the traditional illustrations of the Haggadah is that of Rahel Wischnitzer-Bernstein, "Von der Holbeinbibel zur Amsterdamer Haggadah" in *Monatsschrift fuer Geschichte und Wissenschaft des Judentums*, N.F. vol. 39 (1931), pp. 269-86.

THE SAMARITAN PASSOVER: J. Jeremias, *Die Pasahfeier der Samaritaner* (1932; with many photographs); S. I. Curtiss, *op. cit.*, Appendix F; James A. Montgomery, *The Samaritans* (1907), pp. 37 ff.

THE SONG OF SONGS: A convenient summary of recent theories is: H. H. Rowley, "The Song of Songs: an Examination of Recent Theory," in *Journal of the Royal Asiatic Society*, 1938, pp. 251-76. A new translation of the Song by David de Sola Pool appeared in *The Menorah Journal*, Spring 1945. It is there arranged as a pastoral drama.

PASSOVER CUSTOMS: Many of the customs observed by Jews in connection with Passover are described by H. Schauss, *op. cit.*, pp. 77 ff.

INDEX

ABIMELECH, alliance with Isaac ratified by common meal, 18

Abraham ibn Ezra, on Song of Songs, 88

Addir Hū, Seder hymn, 69

Afikoman, 64

Akiba, Rabbi, on Song of Songs, 88

Angel, escorts Israelites, 41

Anthesteria, laurel and bay at, 19

Aramaic invitation to Seder, 57

Ass, Messianic, Moses rides, 48

BAAL, defeats Yam (Sea), 44

Balmung, Siegfried's weapon, 40

Bitter herbs, 53f.

Blood, smeared on houses or persons: Arabs, Druses, Kurds, Madagascar, Noṣairis (Syria), 21

Blood-smearing, fanciful interpretation of, 49

Bread, unleavened, 18

Bricks, Israelites labor on, legend of, 47

CARPENTRAS, songs from Seder rite of, 74f.

Cohen, name of cake of matzah, 53

Commensality, *see* Eating, Common

Counting Song, at Seder, 70

DARIUS, crossing of Pamphylian Sea by, 42

Dayyenū, Seder hymn, 62

Deliverance, story of, at Seder, 60ff.

Dew, songs for:
   Betalelê ôrah ta'îr adamah, 86
   Lech le-shalôm geshem, 85
   Shelah ruhacha, 85
   Shezufath shemesh, 84

Dew, special prayers for, 84ff.

Door, opening of, during Seder, 65

Drinking, Common, as sign of bond: Luang-Sermata, Madagascar, Nasamoneans, Watubella Islanders, 17

EATING, Common, to cement kinship: Arabs, Kumis (S.E. India), Papuans, Timorlauts, 17

Eating in common with gods: Assyrians, Canaanites, 19

Egg, roasted, 54

Ehad mi yode'a, Seder poem, 70

Elijah, goblet of, 55, 65

Excalibur, magic sword of King Arthur, 40

Exodus:
    date of, 39
    historical background of, 30ff.
    Passover as memorial of, 26

FOUR SONS, section of Haggadah, 59

Four Questions, in Haggadah, 58

Freedom, Season of, 13, 93

GABIROL, Solomon ibn, poems for dew by, 84f.

Garlic, magic use of, 19

Gerizim, Mount, 77

Gibeonites, covenant with Israelites ratified by common food, 18

Gods, annual mourning for: Adonis, Attis, Dionysus, Osiris, Persephone, Tammuz, 25

Goshen, land of, 32

Guide, work on Samaritan religion, 78

Gungnir, magic spear of Odin, 40

HAD GADYÂ, Seder poem, 71

Haggadah, 15
    nucleus of, 56
    passages of, discussed:
        Abadîm hayînū, 58
        Be-chol dôr va-dôr, 63
        Dayyenū, 62
        Four Sons, 58f.
        Hâ lahmâ, 57
        Hallel, 64
        Hasal siddur Pesach, 66
        Kiddush, 57
        Mah nishtanah, 58
        Mi-tehillah, 60
        Ve-hi' she-'omedah, 60
        Zecher la-miqdash ke-Hillel, 64

Hallel, 64

Haroseth, 54

Hasamilis, Hittite god, 42

Haste, in eating paschal meal, 18

Hebrews, identity of, 31

Heliodorus, on ritual limping, 23

Herbs, bitter, 18f.

Herder, on Song of Songs, 89

Hillel, 64

Hyksos, 31

Hyssop, legendary significance of, 49

INDRA, "whizzing bolt" of, 40

Israelite, name of cake of matzah, 53

JACOB ben AARON, Samaritan high priest, 78

Jehovah, 35f.

Jehovah-in-Edom, 36
Jethro, 20

KALIR, Eleazar, liturgical poet, 68
Kenites, 38
Kiddush, 57
Ki lo na'eh, Seder hymn, 68
Kittel, 55, 84
Kinship, sealed by commensality, 18f.

LAMB, why chosen for paschal sacrifice, 49
Leaning posture during Seder, 55, 58
Leaven, removal of, 32
Levite, name of cake of matzah, 53
Limping, ritual: Arabs, Babylonians, Canaanites, Indians, Irish, Tyrians, 23
Limping rhythm of Hebrew dirges, 24
Limping, as rite of mourning, 24
Livy, 42

MAHZOR ROMANIA, 73
Marduk, defeats Tiamat, 44
Matzah, three cakes of, at Seder, 53
Meal, paschal, 13f.
Meal, shared in common, 17f.
Meat, paschal, purity of, 18
Melchizedek, treaty with Abraham ratified by common meal, 18
Merneptah, inscription of, mentioning Israel, 38

Mitzvoth, name for cakes of matzah, 53
Moses:
at the Burning Bush, 27
in the bulrushes, 27
magical credentials of, 28
priestly background of, 35
staff of, 28
Mourning, as seasonal rite, 25

PASCHAL MEAL:
haste in eating of, 18
unleavened bread, 18
bitter herbs, 18f.
purity of meat in, 18
Pasche eggs, 54
Passover:
as confirmation of kinship ties, 18
eighth day of, 15
formal description of, 13ff.
Samaritan, 78ff.
"Season of Freedom," 13, 93
Pesach, as limping rite, 23ff.
Pharaoh, *not* drowned in Red Sea, 30
Pithom and Raamses, 33
Plagues, 28
duration of, 49
Plutarch, on mock funeral in Attis-cult, 25

RAMESSES II, Pharaoh of Exodus, 33
Ransom, as reason for common meals and sprinkling of blood, 22

Red Sea, crossing of, in legend, 50f.

    crossing of, parallels to, 42

    parting of, 43

Rod of Moses, legendary origin of, 47f.

Rod, magic, among Blackfellows, 40

Rumania, mock funeral as seasonal rite in, 25

SABBATH, Passover eve on, 53

Sacrifice, paschal, 14

Samaritans, 77

Seder, 15

    songs of:

        Addir Hū, 69

        Ehad mi yode'a, 70

        Had Gadyâ, 71

        Ki lo na'eh, 68

        Mi-beth aven shebeth medanai, 76

        'Oseh pele' be-Mizraim, 74

        Pesah Mizraim, 73

        U-be-chen va-yehî ba-hazî ha-laylâh, 67

        Va-amartem zebah Pesach, 68

Seder table, articles on, 53f.

Sephardic prayers for dew, 85f.

Serabit el-Khadem, inscriptions, 38

Seti I, Pharaoh of Oppression, 32

Shankbone of lamb, 54

Shepherd, Moses as, 47

Shi 'a Alqûm, god who escorts caravans, 42

Shulamite, the, in Song of Songs, 90

Sojourn in Egypt, story of, at Seder, 60ff.

Song of the Sea (Exodus 15), 51

Song of Songs:

    allegorical interpretation of, 87

    date of, 91

    and Babylonian liturgical chants, 89

        Palestinian love-songs, 91

        as pastoral drama, 89

        read on Passover, 87

Supper, Last, 64

TÂKULTU, Assyrian ceremony, 19

Tell Amarna Letters, on Hebrews (Habiru), 36

Tests of hero, in folktales, 41

Theodore of Mopsuestia, on Song of Songs, 88

Theoxenia, Greek rite, 19

Thornbush, revelation of God in, 47

Tumilat, Wadi, 32

VERVAIN, magic use of, 19

WASHING of hands, at Seder, 57

Wasfs, Syrian songs, 91

Wetzstein, J. G., 90

Wine, cups of, at Seder, 54f.

    sprinkled at enumeration of plagues, 62

YANNAI, liturgical poet, 68